FIRE WALKING

Secrets for Surviving Life's Pressures

Fire Walking
Secrets for Surviving Life's Pressures

Bill L. Little

PEAKE ROAD

Macon, Georgia

ISBN 1-57312-152-5

Fire Walking
Secrets for Surviving Life's Pressures

Bill L. Little

Copyright © 1997

Peake Road
6316 Peake Road
Macon, Georgia 31210-3960
1-800-747-3016

Biblical quotations, unless otherwise noted, are from the
New Revised Standard Version of the Bible (NRSV).

The paper used in this publication
meets the minimum requirements of
American National Standard for Information Sciences—
Permanence of Paper for Printed Library Materials.
ANSI Z39.48–1984

Library of Congress Cataloging-in-Publication

Little, Bill L., 1935–
Fire walking: secrets for surviving life's pressures/
Bill L. Little.
xii + 116 pp.   6" x 9" (15 x 23 cm.)
ISBN 1-57312-152-5 (alk. paper)
1. Christian life—Baptist authors. I. Title.
BV4501.2.L554   1997
248.4'861—dc21   96-37187
                                                            CIP

To my sisters and brother—fellow "fire walkers"
Peggy Sneed
Patsy Williams
Larry Little

Contents

Preface

I had the good fortune of having a lot of unconditional love in my family. That love, especially from my Grandmother Little, gave me a strong foundation for living. By the time I finished high school, I was the most highly educated member of my family, a family of farmers with roots in Mississippi and Southeast Missouri. Married at age eighteen, I was still able to complete college and earn two master's degrees and a doctorate in counseling.

Some of my great thrills have included the publication of three other books, hosting a call-in talk show for CBS radio in St. Louis for seventeen years, and working as team psychologist for the St. Louis Cardinals and the Seattle Mariners. In fact, I was the first psychologist to be hired by a Major League baseball team.

I am a physical fitness nut. I still play basketball, work out on the Nordic Track, and at age fifty-four passed the Marine Corps general fitness test at Camp Pendleton, California.

Life was wonderful for me until I passed my fifty-fifth birthday. At that time, the fires of life began to burn so badly that they scorched my feet. The pain of the last five years has been intense as a result of mistakes I have made, disappointments I have experienced in relationships with people I thought were friends, the end of my marriage, and the death of several significant family members and friends, including my father.

Out of my pain grew these guidelines for surviving the fires of life. They are a compilation of what I have read, heard, thought, and seen. Out of my pain a helpful book has been born. This is an example of a theological concept called "concurrence." It means that God is so much in control of this world that even when bad things are happening to us, there is a parallel activity of God that is producing good to those who are willing to accept it. Because of this, we can know that

Acknowledgments

No book is an island to itself. It is always surrounded by a sea of people who help bring it into being. And this book is certainly no exception. I am indebted to the people whose stories illustrate the guidelines shared here and to those persons who have encouraged me and taught me to see the humor in life.

I learned much about how to love and celebrate living from my late Grandmother Lottie. She loved people and life as much as anyone I have ever known. I learned most of what I know about humor from my father, F. T. Some of his works are included in this book.

There are a lot of other significant thumbprints on the words and on the pages of this book. In recent years I have been encouraged and influenced by a special friend, Gay Carkuson. She patiently listened to each page as it was finished and helped me to clarify ideas and appropriately illustrate them.

There is no way for me to express appreciation to all who have helped me, although I have included comments about some of them in the preface. Many will go unnamed but not unappreciated.

I have constantly been encouraged by my children, Caron, Cheryl, Bill, and Russ. They listen to my ideas, question me, and love me through all my fiery trials.

Certainly I am indebted to Smyth & Helwys for risking the publication of this book. The staff has been consistently helpful, and I am grateful.

To all of the above and many more
Thanks
Bill

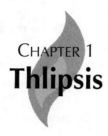

CHAPTER 1
Thlipsis

LIFE BRINGS TO ALL OF US TREMENDOUS PRESSURES. THE GREEKS HAD a word for pressure, *thlipsis* (thlip-sis). Used in the New Testament, it was sometimes translated "affliction." The apostle Paul said he was "afflicted (*thlipsis*) nearly to the point of death" (2 Cor 4:7-9). *Thlipsis* is most graphically pictured by the practice in ancient England of punishing some criminals by placing, one by one, heavy weights on their breasts until they were crushed to death. That is a graphic and symbolic picture of what has happened to many people I have known who have felt the pressures of living. They have nearly been crushed by life.

Demoted: Different Job or *No* Job

Pressure in modern life takes a lot of shapes. One of the most common shapes is a possible job loss or demotion. Many companies are cutting back as a result of pressure in the marketplace or creative automation. As a result, many employees are living with constant stress. They are concerned about the loss of jobs even after years of service with a company. This means no way to pay for a home, children's educations, or retirement.

Five years ago the director of training for a large manufacturer called and asked me to attend an emergency meeting for his company's district sales managers who had twenty to thirty years of service with the company.

"What's the problem?" I asked.

"These people have been with our organization for many years, and now we are asking them to move from managers' jobs back to the sales force. We are also letting a lot of our present sales force go." (I still find the terminology interesting, "letting them go." It almost sounds like they wanted to leave.)

"Demotions, huh?" I thought that was an obvious observation.

"Well," came the response, "We are re-engineering, and it is either a different job or no job at all."

"What do you want me to do?" I had done work for this company several times but had never dealt with this topic except in personal conversations.

"We want you to come in, meet with them for three hours, and make them feel better."

I went. I was not prepared for the level of hostility I met. It was not unlike the meeting I conducted a few years ago for a company on the east coast. That company had a "command" attendance for their managers on a Saturday. It just happened to be the Saturday their state university was playing a football game that could determine the national championship. They were not thrilled about being in a seminar. The "demoted" managers I met were not happy campers.

When I introduced myself to one of the older men there, he responded by saying his name and adding, "I am a TRAINEE." There was no mistaking his tone of voice. He and the other thrity-four new "trainees" were feeling everything from anger and resentment to fear and depression. A week earlier they felt secure in their jobs. Now they felt totally insecure. They had discovered there is no real security in this world except what we carry inside us. They were facing real pressures, and they needed some guidelines.

Same Pressure, Another Face

Don called me at about 9:30 on a rainy night. His voice was filled with tears. He sobbed into the telephone, "Bill, oh Bill, Martha and Stevie have both been killed." His wife and five-year-old son had been in their station wagon. They were hit by a train as Martha tried to cross the tracks. Don was shattered. *Thlipsis!*

I received a telephone call one Sunday morning with news that was to afflict two of my friends. I had to call Alonzo and Retta out of their Sunday School classes and tell them that both of their grandchildren had been killed in an auto accident. They could hardly believe the words. "Are you sure?" They both nearly collapsed. *Thlipsis!*

My friend Lee called me at about 4:30 one morning. "Bill, there has been a terrible accident. Janice has been killed." Janice was his fifteen-year-old daughter. *Thlipsis!*

We all have experienced or will experience these or similar crushing experiences of life. It may come in the form of death, a diagnosis of cancer, or the loss of a job. We all have our burdens to bear. It may be hard to believe, but the same principles that help managers work through losing their positions or jobs can also help people deal with the loss of loved ones through death.

My Own *Thlipsis*

My only two sons were in the Marine Corps and served in the Persian Gulf war. From the time I first got the news that they were both to go there, I felt the pressure. The youngest, Rusty, was an assault team leader with the first division. His group was first to cross into Kuwait. The oldest son, Bill, was an officer with the amphibious force on the Persian Sea.

For six months I watched the news, prayed, worried,and wearily went about my daily routines. When the war ended and both of my sons returned home, it was as if the weights had been lifted off my chest. The tears I had stored in anticipation of a tragic outcome became tears of joy and streamed down my cheeks. I thought I had been through about all the pressure I could stand. I was wrong!

In the year following my sons' return, my only uncle (like a second father to me) died of cancer in the liver and pancreas. About four months later, on a Saturday in February, with no prior announcement, my wife of thirty-eight years served me with divorce papers. On the same afternoon, my father (and best friend) had a stroke. My uncle died. My marriage ended. My father died. *Thlipsis!*

I was pressed down, but somehow not overcome. Life continued. My energy drained. My creativity was reduced. I continued to function and work through it without falling into deep depression, however. I kept going.

Now, years later, I am reflecting over how I made it through that time of increasing, terrible pressure. I know the grace of God was involved, and yet I have known others with the same grace who have become incapacitated by even less pressure. No matter what the source of the pressure, the principles for dealing with it are the same.

What Makes the Difference?

The difference in how people deal with pressure and crisis is probably a result of a combination of things. Perhaps role models have been stronger for some. Perhaps some strength of personality comes from genetic inheritance. Perhaps some of the ability to cope comes from general physical conditioning. I am confident that all of these things are involved, but there is more.

A major part of our ability to cope effectively and positively with the times of pressure in our lives is a result of beliefs and skills developed and learned through our struggles. We are all capable of dealing with life through greater strength. We can learn the attitude that will enable us to do as Beethoven did when he was going deaf. He said, "I will take life by the throat." He did, and he more than coped. He continued to produce great music.

I firmly believe we can learn to do more than cope with life. We can continue to produce music in our lives even during the hard times. We can continue to live in the face of adversity. Life will periodically be colored by suffering but, as one sufferer said, "I purpose to choose the color."

Is all of this important? You bet it is! As Scott Peck so eloquently pointed out, life is difficult. He says this fact may be the one of the greatest truths we will ever discover. Because life is difficult for all of us, we all need basic coping skills.

Difficult, stressful, challenging, but manageable—this is life on planet Earth. I love the statement from Rollo May about freedom. He said, "Freedom is the ability to pause between a stimulus and a response and in that pause to make a decision." That makes life manageable for me. When I am faced with a pressure, I can at least pause and make a decision.

People who are being demoted can stop in the middle of the experience and ask themselves how they want to respond. People who are facing the death of a loved one can even stop during the horrible time and ask the same question. The problem is, decisions are only as good as our information. Some people have never learned that they have choices. They have few skills to call on when they are faced with the pressures of life.

This book is about the development of coping skills, the changing of belief systems to embrace laws that will guide and empower us to tap into our internal, God-given strengths. Embracing these laws will permit us to become more than conquerors, even in life's most devastating moments.

Biblical Reaction to *Thlipsis*

Perhaps the Psalms best reflect the most clear reactions to life's pressures. Look at these words: "Give ear to my words, O Lord; give heed to my sighing. Listen to the sound of my cry, my King and my God" (5:1-2). Note: these are the words of suffering, but also note, the writer never lost hope. Even in the midst of suffering, he wrote, "my King and my God."

Even more graphic words appear in Psalm 6:6, "I am weary with my moaning; every night I flood my bed with tears; I drench my couch with my weeping." Those words were written by someone who had experienced *thlipsis*. I remain impressed by the fact that even in the times of pressure, the biblical writers never lost courage and hope. They did more than just survive.

More Than Just Surviving

Life is lived on at least three levels. (1) non-functioning, or the inability to work or relate; (2) functioning; and (3) transcending, or rising above it all and living with internal energy and vision. Between these levels of living we go through what may best be called "transitions." We move from one level to another, most of the time unconsciously.

We can move beyond functioning. We can get above just transacting business through the force of our wills. We can make the transition to transcendent living. We can have energy, creativity, productivity, sanity, and better health. We can live by our own internal values with power and purpose if we apply certain guidelines to our lives. We can make conscious decisions to make those applications. This is what the Greeks called *hupomone* (who-pa-moan-e). It implied a lot more than grim, bleak acceptance of the afflictions of life. It meant enduring with courage until personal victory came (1 Cor 1:6; Col 1:11).

The patient courage to endure and overcome whatever circumstances we face is built on a set of skills, attitudes, and lifestyle that can be taught and learned. I want to share with you the ideas and beliefs that have enabled me and many others to be more than survivors through difficult times. These beliefs have helped me, in my saner moments, to be content with whatever circumstances I have faced in life (Phil 4:4-13).

If we learn and adopt more powerful beliefs, we can join the victors in seeing joy in life even when we walk under the weight of pressures. We can have enduring courage sufficient for every affliction. That may be what matters most in living!

CHAPTER 2
What Is Reality?

FOR AT LEAST A QUARTER OF A CENTURY I HAVE BEEN INTRIGUED BY Hans Viahinger's philosophy of fictional finalism. As I understand his theory, it means we all live with our own personal view of the world. This is called our "fiction," not because it is false, but because it doesn't matter whether it is true or not. What matters is that we believe it because we will live as if it is true anyway. To us, our beliefs are true.

I came across this concept when I was reading a book by Anthony Robbins called *Unlimited Power*. There I read of the "lies of success." They are called lies because it doesn't matter whether these ideas concerning success are true or not. They are truth for the people who believe them and act on them.

The concepts concerning fictional finalism and the lies of success are important, but keep in mind: Facts are not the issue; perception is! This does not mean that facts are unimportant. I may perceive that I can fly. The fact is, I cannot. If I ignore the fact, I can leap into the air from a tall building and become no more than a blot on the pavement. Perception will not change the fact. Perception will determine how we respond to the facts.

Perhaps the concept will be more clear if we think about the beliefs of paranoid people. When such people believe that others are out to get them, their belief becomes reality. It doesn't matter to paranoid persons that others believe there is no evidence to support their suspicious view. Those people will live as if their belief is true. It becomes a "fictional finalism."

I sometimes call this the "as if" philosophy. We live as if our beliefs are true, and thus, for us, they are true. We see this idea reflected in various words and phrases. The Bible, for example, teaches that as we think, so we are.

Motivational speakers are heard saying things such as, "No one ever performs consistently in a manner inconsistent with his/her self-concept." What we believe about ourselves determines most of what we do and most of what we become.

We behave in ways and reflect attitudes that are consistent with our deepest and strongest beliefs. These deep beliefs are our "fictional finalisms." We live according to the laws and guidelines that make up our deep belief systems. When we add these "laws" to our belief systems, we change our abilities to cope with life.

But What If I Lose My Job?

What I believe about myself and my abilities will have a lot to do with not only how I feel, but also how well I do in finding something else to do. I can begin by saying to myself that I may never find another job as good as this one. I know of a situation where a sixty-year-old engineer was told his job was being terminated. He was in a state of shock. He couldn't even clean out his desk without help. He literally cried and said aloud, "I will never be able to find another job. I'm too old to find work. I don't know how I am going to make it."

His belief system is creating a miserable reality for him. He is not bound to that perception, however. He can consciously make a decision to change it. He could say, "This is not a pleasant situation, but I am a survivor. I am a capable person who has a lot of friends. I will probably find a job right after I return from the extended vacation I've been putting off. This is an opportunity for me to find out just how good I am."

If he can learn techniques for putting those beliefs into his deepest thought system, his perception will be a pleasant one, and he will enhance his chances for finding a good job. This principle applies to every area of life.

One Woman's Deep Beliefs

She is a very attractive lady, about forty-five, a redhead who dresses well and always seems proper in behavior. If you meet her on the street, Lucy will not appear unusual. She will appear to be just like anyone else on the way to work or going shopping. She is different, however. She has a life-threatening cancer.

I asked her, "Why do you want to live?" She responded softly, "I can't think of any reason." Lucy proceeded to tell me that she does not believe she is important to anyone. "No one really cares what happens to me, except when they need something from me."

Her beliefs are almost totally negative and debilitating. If I or someone else cannot help her to change these deep negative beliefs, she will die prematurely. I wish for a way to mechanically open up her mind, remove all the destructive thoughts and replace them with positive, empowering ones. As yet, this is not possible, so we go about this life-saving task in the only way we know. We retrain the mind, one step, one thought, one belief at a time.

There Is a Way

People can beat cancer and other illnesses. Some conventional and unconventional treatments have worked, but they seldom work unless the patient has powerful and empowering coping skills grounded in positive beliefs.

It is possible to face the loss of a marriage, the death of a loved one, the loss of a job, the devastation of floods or storms, or the loss of money and still live happy and productive lives. All we need is patient endurance to be victorious. We need mental and emotional toughness, the ability to live with power—which we can develop.

A Simple But Not Easy Answer

The ability to live with power, regardless of outward circumstance, is based on three simple realities: (1) saying positive, powerful things about ourselves both to ourselves (self-talk grounded in our inner beliefs) and to others (the verbalizations of our inner beliefs), (2) doing positive and empowering things (acting out our beliefs), and (3) believing positive, powerful things about ourselves and our world (our deepest and strongest beliefs).

The third of these is probably the most important. We may be able to say the "right" things for a while, even if we don't believe them. That helps but, after a while, saying alone isn't enough. Unless we can bring harmony between what we say outwardly and what we believe inwardly, we will soon know that we are just spouting empty words.

What We Say Is Important

Make no mistake about it. Saying positive things is a thousand percent better than saying negative things to yourself and to others, but it isn't enough. We can use our internal and external verbalizations to help us change behavior, feelings, and ultimately our deepest beliefs. But unless we are successful in making those deeper changes, we will simply run out of energy.

An illustration from an old form of power might be helpful. If a steam engine operator uses all the power to blow the whistle (outward expression) but has nothing left to run the engine (inner drive, grounded in deep belief), little work can be done.

I am not among those who believe that talk is meaningless. Words are powerful. Just look at history. Were the words of Lincoln at Gettysburg powerful? How about the words of Martin Luther King, Jr. in his famous "I Have a Dream" speech in Washington, D.C.? Hitler used words to lead a nation into a mad attempt to conquer the world. Roosevelt challenged America with the simple words, "The only thing we need fear, is fear itself."

Words have been used to destroy relationships, character, churches, businesses, and even nations. Words have been used to encourage and save people and institutions. Caution: what you say to yourself and to others will impact your life. You might read from the book of James that the tongue, though a small member of the body, can start terrible fires. Like the small rudder of a ship, the tongue directs our lives. What we say, in large measure, determines our direction.

Names are also powerful words. Beware of calling yourself, your children, and others negative and destructive names (for example, Slow, Dumb, Stupid, Ugly, Mean, and Ignorant). Such words and those that reflect our beliefs are tremendously important. We will be well advised to change our negative names and words into positive ones. While verbalizations (words) are very important, they cannot stand alone to empower us for dealing with the afflictions of life.

Behavior Is Important

When I say that acting is not enough, I am not saying that behavior is unimportant. The contrary is true. How we act, especially when we face tough problems, is very important. Our outward behavior must eventually be consistent with what we really believe deep inside ourselves, or it will drain us of needed energy.

There are times when I advocate "fake it until we can make it," but only until we can make it. We can "act" strong only for a limited amount of time. I frequently see people who are tired of being strong. They really want to "let down" for a while.

Karen and James came to my office just a few days after she had been diagnosed with breast cancer. They were uncommonly calm and collected for people who were facing such a difficult situation. At one point, James took her hand in his and said to me, "She will be fine. She is a very strong person." She smiled weakly and nodded. I said, "Karen, aren't you tired of being strong?" She burst into tears, "Oh, God, yes!" It was almost as if she was waiting for permission to stop being strong for a little while. She eventually regained her strength and is doing very well in her treatment program.

Again, behaving in positive ways and exhibiting a positive attitude is almost always better than the opposite. Still the behavior will become a burden to us unless we can build it on a foundation of solid and deep beliefs. Perhaps Henry George said it best, "When there is correct thought, right action will follow."

Feelings Are Not Good or Bad

I believe in the honest expression of feelings. This does not mean I believe in expressing all feelings. In some situations it is inappropriate to express feelings, but even those situations do not rule out finding appropriate and helpful ways of expressing emotions. Emotions are wonderful as support and affirmation for us. They do not, however, make the most reliable leaders in life. If we follow our feelings and only do what we "feel" like doing, we will never do a lot of very important things.

While it is vital to get in touch with our feelings, to know them, to be able to verbalize them, to not fear them, it is also important not to permit them to control our lives. Dogs and other lower animal forms seem to do pretty much what they feel like doing when they feel like doing it. Human beings have the ability to rise above negative feelings and choose positive responses.

A feeling is not good or bad. It is just a feeling. Emotions make wonderful allies but dangerous masters. Feelings are helpful as guides and affirmations of inner beliefs, but not enough to dictate either our actions or our beliefs.

Deep Beliefs Are the Key

Ultimately, our perception determines our reality. How we think determines what we are. What we believe determines how we act, how we feel, and what we say. Our belief systems, reflected in our self-talk, make up the foundations for life skills. We cannot build strong living skills without changing our inner beliefs.

Beliefs control us, even when we are not aware of it. An example comes from my own life experience. Until a few years ago, I felt guilty about buying shoes. It didn't matter what they cost nor how much money I had. I couldn't figure out why I felt guilty until I asked myself an appropriate question. (Our minds answer the questions we ask of them.) I simply asked, "Why do I feel guilty about buying shoes?" The answer was simple. When I was growing up, I must have heard at least 736 times, "Bill, take care of your shoes. If you are just going to play, take your shoes off and go barefoot. Save your shoes for Sunday and for school. We can't afford new shoes."

I had taps, half-soles, and heels put on my shoes because "we couldn't afford shoes." Time passed and my situation changed, but the basic belief that I could not afford shoes was still lying in my subconscious mind. From its bed in my subconscious, my belief was controlling me and generating guilt. I could go to St. Louis International Airport and buy a ticket for Athens, Greece, and not feel guilt. It never occurred to my family to tell me that we couldn't afford tickets to Athens.

What we believe is true whether it is or not. I had an uncle who believed in predestination (theological determinism). He believed it to the point that my grandfather used to say of him, "He believes that what is to be will be whether it is or not." That is true of our beliefs.

They are true simply because we believe them. To paraphrase a Scripture passage about thinking, "As you believe in your heart, so are you."

We find a way to rationalize our beliefs, even when facts get in the way. My predestinarian uncle could always rationalize his belief. One morning he strapped on a six-gun and started out the door of his East Texas home. His wife asked, "Why are you taking that gun with you?" He explained that he was going to walk out in a pasture and "there may be some rattlesnakes out there." She thought she had him. She mockingly said, "Well, if it is to be that a snake is going to bite you, it will bite you whether you have a gun or not." She smiled. He was undaunted. Without hesitating he said, "Yes, but if it is to be that I am to shoot it, I'll need a gun."

Our beliefs are so deep and strong, they control our lives. They determine our attitudes and actions. Our beliefs are also not easily changed. We really must decide to change them and work toward the change.

The Source of Power

When we bring together our deepest beliefs, our feelings, our actions, and our verbalizations in a positive and empowering concert, we will live with power. The purpose of this book is to share the techniques that enable us to control our internal beliefs and then to apply those techniques to adopt for ourselves some healthy, positive, and powerful beliefs.

Through repetition, exercise, explanation, and example, I hope to help you develop some guidelines for living that I have found helpful. I want you to sink them deep into your mind. If you change your mind, you will change your life!

CHAPTER 3
Laws for
Walking Through the Fires

LIVING THROUGH THE PRESSURES OF LIFE CAN BE COMPARED TO walking through fire. Once I really did walk through coals of fire. It was part of a seminar I attended. The experience of walking barefoot across a bed of hot coals was supposed to symbolize overcoming some personal fear. I understood the point and walked without being burned, but I am still afraid to walk on fire.

Afraid or not, there are plenty of times we are all called on to walk through some kind of fire in life. I have made it through thus far. Oh, I can smell a little burnt hair, and there is the smell of smoke in my clothes, but I have made it so far.

The Old Testament prophet Isaiah believed that if we have faith in God, we can walk through the fire and not be burned. He didn't promise that we won't feel the heat, just that we won't be burned. I can't promise that you will not get a little burned at times, but I can share with you some guidelines for making it through life's hot spots. I call these "Little's Laws for Walking Through Fire." I discuss each of these "laws" in the following chapters. They form what I believe will be a helpful core of beliefs for living through pressures and afflictions.

Perseverance
Keep On Walking

I have learned an important rule in my fire walks (both the literal and the symbolic): Keep walking! A surefire way to get burned is to stop walking. When I am afraid, I walk on. When I am hurting, I walk on. When I feel the heat under my feet, I walk on. As a result, I have made it through up to the present. I may not have made it through in the best way. I may have made it through in the worst way. That is not the issue for me at the moment. I just know that I have made it through.

Looking back at my divorce, the death of my uncle, the death of my dad, and some real disappointments with people, I have asked, "How did I make it through all that?" The most significant thing I did was simply to keep on walking.

I remember what I said when Don told me about the death of his wife and five-year-old son, Stevie. I prayed all the way as I drove to meet with him. I knew it would be a horrible time for him, and I wanted to help. I will never forget the tearful question, "Both of them, Bill. Oh God, both of them. How can I make it?" I groped for words. "I don't know, Don. I think there are times that the only thing any of us can do is just put one foot in front of the other. There are no answers I can give you for a time like this. You just have to walk on through the pain and tears. All I can do is walk with you as far as I can."

I have probably given that advice hundreds of times since then. I gave it to the couple who lost their grandchildren in a car wreck. I gave that advice to Lee, whose daughter was killed in another auto accident. I gave it to a man whose wife was burned to death in a fire that destroyed their home. I have given that advice to people diagnosed with cancer. I give that advice to myself, "Just keep on putting one foot in front of the other. Persevere."

The application is made to everything that produces pressure in life. When I talk with people who are facing the possibility of being caught in the process of downsizing within their company, I know they are under constant stress. Sometimes there is a tendency to just back away, to quit. It is easier to just "not go on." If you face that kind of pressure, the same concepts can help you that help people deal with catastrophic loss. Just keep doing your job to the best of your ability. Put one foot in front of the other and walk on.

Patience
This Time Will Pass

When we are in the middle of a crises, when we are feeling the weight of affliction, when emotional pain is almost unbearable, it seems that time will never end.

I have been critical of people who have walked up to a suffering person and said, "This will pass. In time you will feel better." I've thought, "But they are hurting right now, so who cares if someday it will be better." I have learned that as empty as those words may sound, however, they are true. Remember, pain is time-limited. If we can see a possible end, we can make it through most things. Even life is a time-limited problem. It has a beginning and an end. The more clearly I see this, the easier it is to press on through the fires of life. This is a practical concept. We can use it even in the lesser problems.

I recently had surgery on my right knee. (It was my "good" knee). When I felt the pain, I reminded myself that it would soon be over. It helped. The same logic can be applied while sitting in a dentist's chair. "Just a few more minutes. I know I can make it for a few more minutes." That doesn't solve the problem, but it does encourage us.

Knee surgery and tooth pain are minor compared to what many people are going through. These are only little sparks. Some people are walking through enormous flames. Perhaps it will encourage them to know that if they just keep on walking, the time will pass, and the pain will become less. It may end all together. Be patient. "Let patience have her perfect work" (Jas 1:4 KJV).

Positive Outcome
Make It Work for You

A rough paraphrase of an often-repeated verse from the Bible is "everything works for you." Not everything is good. Only a few pompous folks who are in complete denial would say that everything is good. There are a lot of genuinely awful things in life, but they can be made to work for us. Some of the gains are small in comparison to the pain, but since the pain is there anyway, I might as well gain something. My pain has at least made me a little more sensitive to the pain of others. I am more empathetic as a result of my own suffering.

The fires of life are not cooled by the knowledge that they will eventually cook up something good. Rather, the knowledge that we can find something positive, even in a tragedy, gives us a little more strength to make it through our time of pain. Looking for a way to make something positive happen gives us a different focus at a time when we really need one.

There have been situations where people were locked into a job and would never have left unless they were forced out. We certainly can do a lot more than we think we can when the pressure is there. Necessity is indeed the mother of invention and inventive actions. Forced out of a job where they were literally "trapped," people have found wonderful new directions in life.

I have never been comforted by the "Pollyanna" spirit or words. The fact that things will work for good does not ease the pain we experience in the present, but it does give us hope and courage to keep on going. Find a way to make it work for you.

Contentment
Take What Is and Make the Most of It

"Make lemonade from your lemons. Find the solutions behind the problems." This is not new information for you. I hope this concept has become part of your internal belief system because, if we enter the fires with the belief that we can take whatever is and make the most of it, we will be encouraged to keep on walking.

I am not saying that I will take what is and make it perfect. I have learned the futility of such effort. Human perfection is an illusion promoted by some psychotherapists and religious fundamentalists. It does not exist in our real world, and those who lead us to believe that it does are doing us a horrible injustice. Still we are constantly raising expectations to unrealistic heights simply because it "sells." As a result, many people will fall from these unrealistic altitudes and be crushed in the process.

Pop psychology culture and talk show mentality do a great disservice to our societal psyche. To deny or ignore the pain in life and to replace it with a "whistle while you work" attitude is both unrealistic and unhealthy. It is no great revelation that repressed feelings later surface as larger dragons to slay. As we sit and wait for the coals to cool, the fire only gets hotter. Life can be good, life can be fun; but make no mistake about it, life is not perfect.

The closest we can come to perfection is in our direction or goals. We are not called upon to create perfection from our situations, only to make the most of them. As we make the most of what is, we may find enough joy and courage to make it through without wasting our time in ceaseless complaining.

Problems and flaws will always exist. The problem-free life is a myth, but the ability to find meaning and joy is real. I believe I have made it thus far in life, in part, because I honestly believe that I can take whatever is and make the most of it, all in the spirit of celebration.

Responsibility
Clean Up Your Own Trash

Stand on your own feet. True fire walkers ride on no one's shoulders. They walk on their own feet. Maybe this law has been obscured by modern psychology, law, and even theology. For too long we have been led to believe that we can blame something or someone for our own problems and our inability to handle them. We have created what Charles Sykes refers to in his book, *A Nation of Victims,* as a "nation of victims."

We are eager to believe that murderers must have some uncontrollable psychological problem, or they would not have committed such a heinous crime. Perhaps it comforts us to think that such behavior is "sick." Well, I *am* sick. I am sick and tired of seeing people being encouraged to blame society, family background, genetic inheritance, race, sex, childhood abuse, and the devil for their own weaknesses and inability to cope. How in the world does that help anyone make it through a crisis?

Of course we had problems when we were growing up. Some of us were spanked or even seriously abused. Some have been sexually abused. Some have been raised in poor and deprived families. We cannot, however, afford the luxury of remaining victimized by any of these things. We can choose to live for the rest of our lives as emotional cripples who can never do well or have the strength to make it through the trials of life because so many "horrible" things have happened to us. There is another choice, however.

We can rise above our backgrounds. We can deal with life on the basis of our own responsibility. I cannot control what has happened to me, but I can control my response to what is happening now. Only when we assume personal responsibility for living do we really live. Only then are we able to walk through the fires and survive. No matter what our backgrounds racially, economically, psychologically, religiously, or sexually, we will not be helped by blaming the past for our inability to live in the present. Courage comes from assuming personal responsibility.

Most of us can be helped by the advice given by my friend, Jim White, to whiners: "DWI—deal with it." We need to deal with life for ourselves when it is possible—and it usually is. My son, Bill, calls this sense of responsibility "cleaning up your own mess." The Bible teaches that we can no longer blame our sins on our parents. The soul that sins will die. We are responsible.

Integrity
Be True to You

We will have a lot more strength for facing the ordeals of life if we have maintained the courage to be true to our own values. Nothing saps more energy than pretense. Hypocrisy destroys internal energy.

Living with peer pressure tempts one to sacrifice personal value in order to be accepted by the group. Once the process begins, it is like an avalanche. It results in checking with others for every decision, even about clothing. After a while, we produce a condition called incongruence. What is inside no longer is consistent with what is outside.

This concept of incongruence is illustrated in a book written by Glenn Clark, *I Will Lift Up Mine Eyes,* in which he points out the power of bringing together our conscious and subconscious minds. Conversely, there is very little energy in a person who is incongruent. Integrity empowers us for facing the pressures of life. If you want to have to the strength to keep on walking, you had better walk your own walk. Be true to the best you.

Gratitude
Be Gladder Than Madder

It is amazing how the expression of gratitude calms the soul and clears the mind. The next time you feel anxious, remember this. Peace cannot be produced by willing it. Try it. Say to yourself, "Now I am going to feel peaceful. No matter what is happening, I am going to feel peace." Does that work for you? I doubt it.

The fact is, peace is usually a byproduct. The way to produce peace is to focus on peaceful things. Start by listing all the things for which you are thankful. When faced with a crisis, decisions and actions are much more helpful when they are generated out of an inner calm and confidence, enhanced by a spirit of gratitude.

Complaining about losses solves nothing. When looking at the things his family had lost, Gerald Mann, in *When the Bad Times Are Over,* exhorted his wife and children, "Be gladder that we had them than madder that we lost them." Be gladder than madder. That attitude enabled the family to make it through enormous pressure. No wonder the apostle Paul admonished, "In everything . . . with thanksgiving let your requests be known to God" (Phil 4:6).

Humor
Have as Much Fun as You Can

Years ago I read a book titled *How Never to Be Tired.* It emphasized that the way to keep your energy up is to learn how to enjoy whatever you have to do. There is no question that the anticipation of fun elevates the level of energy. There is also no question that energy is required for walking through the fires of life.

I can be dragging at the end of a day. I feel like what one of my friends used to describe as being beaten with a "tired stick." It still astounds me that I experience an immediate rise in energy if someone comes by and wants to go to the gym for a game of one-on-one basketball. I love to play basketball. The anticipation of fun raises the level of my energy.

I also love to laugh. Laughter is healthy. Norman Cousins certainly proved that. He laughed his way through the pain of life-threatening illness.

My father seemed to have a lot of energy even though he worked long hours. I asked him about his approach. He said, "Well, Bill, I would rather not work at all, but someone messed this world up long before I arrived on the scene, so I have to work. Since I have to work, I have decided to enjoy it as much as I can. I have quite a lot of fun at work." He did and he had a wonderful sense of humor, which helped him through a lot of crises. I call it my seventh sense, my sense of humor. Have as much fun as you can.

Celebration
Create Moments for Yourself

I have learned that I can celebrate life, even in the bad times. The hard times are made easier when I focus on celebration. This does not mean that I am celebrating the pain or the problems. I am celebrating life even in the midst of the fire.

It is said that some of the early Christian martyrs died in the flames of persecution while singing hymns. No doubt some died while screaming in pain. It was a choice. The heroic saints knew they were going to die. It was simply a matter of how. They chose to die celebrating their faith. That didn't stop the dying, but it made it more bearable for them.

I am not being too drastic when I suggest that we learn to celebrate. Singing is one way I have learned to celebrate. I have learned to sing, no matter what is happening to me. I don't always feel like singing, and I don't sing automatically when I am hit with a crisis. I just know that somewhere deep within myself the songs are still there.

I find myself singing more and more as I grow older—which means I am singing quite a lot. I believe music is one of the great gifts of the church. In that ritual a truth has shined through my clouded mind. I can sing in the darkness of affliction. It is even more effective than whistling.

When I am afraid, I sing, "I will not be afraid. I will not be afraid. I will look upward and travel onward and not be afraid." It honestly helps me to make it through my fear. When I am discouraged, I sing again and again the refrain, "The joy of the Lord is my strength."

Think about it. What has empowered people such as Martin Luther King, Jr. to make it through the fires of injustice? Was it not, at least in part, his ability to sing, "We shall overcome, we shall overcome someday"?

In painful moments we can find things to celebrate if we look within our souls. I do not mean to imply that we are to be happy about the pain or pressure. I am just saying that we can learn to look beyond the dark moment into the light of joy and celebration.

Part of walking through the fire is dependent on my inner beliefs. These beliefs were learned and nurtured in my family, in school, in church, in reading, and in my relationships. The belief that I can create a moment of celebration even in the hard times is important to me. I have made it through the fires in my life partly because I have learned to look for ways to celebrate.

Internal Control
Stay in Your Own Circle

We cannot control what happens to us, but we can choose the frames we put around our experiences. We can give our own slant to the events of life without denying the reality of those events.

Years ago I wrote, "Even if fate deals you a crummy hand, you can still choose how to play it." Jesus Christ taught that it is not what goes into the body that defiles it, but what is inside. From the heart evil or good proceeds. Whether good or evil, it depends on the view from inside. We can control the internal system of beliefs and attitudes that in turn controls the external results.

Stephen Covey develops some helpful ideas on the concept of internal control. He draws a small circle inside a larger one. He points out that the events in the large circle are outside our control. The events in the smaller circle are in our control. Most of our worry and fear is a result of living too much of our time in the outer circle. We accomplish a lot more and are able to deal more effectively, even with major problems, when we stay in the circle of control.

I have learned to ask myself about life situations, "Is this in my circle of control?" If it is not, I ask myself, "Then what can I do that is in my circle of control?" I always feel better and accomplish more when I operate within my circle of control. This law may be stated in terms of focus. When we remain focused, we can stay in the area of our own control. It is a choice. I choose to focus on the things over which I have some measure of control.

Passion
Be Enthusiastic

It is astounding to see the difference that enthusiasm makes in the level of energy we have. Enthusiasm literally means, "God in us." It generates a feeling of passion for life. Young people often talk about things that really "turn them on." I think we are wise to ask ourselves if we are turned on to life. We can be! Passion turns the "daily grind" into the "daily grand."

I am not talking about the kind of enthusiasm produced by a charismatic speaker, the kind of hype that leaves you feeling as if you can overcome anything—that is, until you step outside the meeting and get splashed by muddy water by a passing auto. That shallow passion dies long before we walk through the fire. I am talking about the kind of passion that grows out of deep beliefs and commitments. We can learn lasting excitement.

It is not easy to develop this kind of enthusiasm, but it can be done. And it is certainly worth the effort. There will be plenty of obstacles to overcome, but we can work our way through them easier if we have developed a passion for life.

Love
Learn to Love Life

Years ago Lawrence LaShan told me that the only valid reason for living is that we want to live. When we love living, we are energized to fight through the fires and keep on living. Our immune systems are looking to us for a reason to fight. When we tell them we want them to fight because we have so many duties to fulfill and so many responsibilities to meet, it does little to empower those systems. But when we tell our immune systems we want them to fight for our lives because we really love living, they are empowered.

No doubt love is the strongest emotion in the world. Maybe when we develop the ability to walk on, give thanks, have fun, be true to ourselves, and celebrate life, we will fall in love with living. As a result, we can walk through the fires with assurance.

Foundations

The Master Builder said the foundation of the house is vital. If we build on the sand, when the storms or fires come, the structure will fall. If we build on the rock, when the storms or fires come, the house will stand.

All of the guidelines in this chapter are valid. They are not all the guidelines for living, but they are enough to help us through most

24

situations. They will not stand, however, unless they are grounded in two very important foundation rocks: health and faith.

We need to stay physically fit, mentally fresh, and socially active and to maintain healthy habits. We can apply all twelve "laws" to our lives, but if we destroy ourselves with bad habits and fail to stay fit, the structure will fall.

Likewise, life can never be abundant and victorious without an internal strength grounded in a belief in something beyond us. It might start with a belief in a cosmic force or a great cause. For me, it is faith in God. Faith in God provides a foundation from which I develop the ability to apply the guidelines for walking through the fires. That faith is unconditional. It is as binding as a marriage contract. I have faith during the good times and the bad times. I can do all things through Christ.

The importance of faith is generally accepted even in treatment programs for alcoholism. In AA (Alcoholics Anonymous), it is called believing in "your higher power." Someone has said, "If we haven't that within us which is above us, we will soon yield to that which is around us."

Without a foundation of health and faith we will build on the sand, and the superstructure will fall around us. With the foundation we will be able to walk on with courage.

Maintain Quality

If I have learned to live on the higher levels of life, I can maintain high quality living no matter what is happening around me. We waste a lot of energy by focusing on the externals. These are ususaly things over which we have no control. Life is enriched when we move the focus to the things in our circle of control. I can control my attitude. I can control my actions. I can control my choice to apply the laws for walking through the fires of life.

CHAPTER 4

How Do We Get There from Here?

LAWS OR GUIDELINES ARE USELESS UNLESS WE ARE ABLE TO ADOPT them as our very own. We create most of our own reality, but we can change what we create. Archimedes said, "Give me a lever long enough . . . and single-handedly I can move the world." If we can discover the right levers, we can change the way we think and what we believe, and thus change our world.

In the last chapter I shared with you "Little's Laws for Walking Through the Fires." Now I want to share with you some methods for incorporating these laws into your own belief system. The remaining chapters of this book deal with the "laws" individually. I hope you will adopt the most helpful of these "laws," and they will become part of your deepest and strongest beliefs.

Metanoia

The Greek word *metanoia* comes from two words, *meta,* meaning "above or beyond," and *nous,* meaning "mind." The combined word means a shift of mind. It was translated in the New Testament as "repent."

Repentance means a complete turnaround. If you were traveling north and repented, you would be traveling south. One way we effect the changing of minds (*metanoia*) is through education. Real education changes our minds and thus produces changes in our attitudes and actions. According to Peter Senge, writing in *The Fifth Discipline,* through learning we can re-create ourselves and change life; we can do things we could not do previously and perceive the world and our relationship to it differently.

Change Is a Choice

A second way to effect change in our minds is through choice. I can decide to change a concept and deliberately set out to make the change. For example, I might be afraid of heights. I can decide to shift my thinking. As a result of the choice, I can practice by desensitizing myself to heights. This may be accomplished by gradually working my way upstairs and talking to myself as I get higher. Self-talk can include the repetition of a new belief. I can say, "I am becoming less afraid of heights." After repeating the statement until I am comfortable while climbing a few stairs, I could add a stronger statement such as, "I am no longer afraid of heights." Whatever works for me is what I will use.

I can also choose to act as if I am changing. I can face the fear and do the fearful anyway. I can get on an elevator even when I am afraid. If I do that often enough, I can change my belief as I change my action.

Repeat New Beliefs of Laws

We change a belief by frequent repetition. The repetition of a new idea can take the form of self-talk. I can say something to myself over and over. "I believe that things work for me. I believe that things work for me. I believe that things work for me. . . ." I can also write the belief on cards and stick them on mirrors, doors, sun visors in my car, or on my desk. When I see what I have written, I repeat it to myself. I can also make audiotapes of my voice repeating beliefs I want to adopt. Then I can listen to them as I go to sleep or as I drive. If I really want to adopt healthier and stronger beliefs, I must pay the price of discipline.

Change Can Come by Default

Mind-changing also takes place as a result of necessity. I may believe that I am going to be in a certain relationship until I die only to be faced with the death of the partner or a divorce. Unless I am in complete denial, I will have to change my belief.

How did we get here? We all have deep belief systems. We accumulated them over the years. We may or may not know how we developed those beliefs. They have been a part of our life experience.

It is almost as if we have been brainwashed by life experiences and have never realized there was any other way.

Some of our accumulated beliefs are helpful and, in fact, powerful coping beliefs. Because we arrived at some good places in our belief systems does not mean we necessarily know how to build on those concepts and develop better ones.

Is it insight or a conscious change of beliefs? When my oldest son, Bill, was in freshman algebra, he turned in a notebook with answers to the problems he had been given in class. I was called to come to school and talk with Bill and his teacher. The math teacher explained to me that he was giving Bill a failing grade on the notebook because he had not worked out the problems. My son asked if the answers were right. He was told they were, but he needed to show how he had gotten them. The method was as important as the answer.

When Bill turned in the second notebook, he got something like a 96% for his work. The problem he missed was marked with the comment, "You have used the right method, but you got the wrong answer." Bill wanted to know which the teacher really wanted, right answers or right methods? I told him he would find it important to get both.

While it is possible to arrive at the best place without knowing how we got there, it is important for us to learn the methods by which we may achieve *metanoia*. We may want to develop new concepts that will give us stronger systems with which to live victoriously.

Let's Talk

In the remainder of this book I use the same concepts we use in conversation. I share laws or guidelines for walking through the fires of life and then restate the law in terms of a belief. Following the statement of the law (belief), I discuss the belief with stories and illustrations. I then challenge us all to make the decision to adopt the belief or law if we find it helpful. We can do that through the methods described above, especially through repetition. I ask that we use paraphrases, mottos, and even create our own fictions about how we can implement the belief or law. If I describe a belief that is already a part of your belief system, you may want to read the chapter for affirmation or perhaps for new ways to implement the belief.

If the chapter begins with a law that is not a part of your own belief system, then use the law to help you get in touch with your own belief. You might believe just the opposite of what I do. Is what you already believe working effectively for you? Would this new idea be more effective? If so, use the concepts in the rest of the chapter to help you achieve *metanoia,* a change of mind.

I call these guidelines laws, not because they are written in granite, or even on stone tablets, but because they have been helpful to me. I hope you will at least look them over with an open mind. In each chapter I give a description of the effects the law or guideline has on life, using illustrations from the lives of people who have exercised the law. The purpose of this section is clarification, for when we see examples in the lives of others, we understand the impact of a concept much more vividly.

Commitment

If you really want to impact your life with these ideas, you are confronted with a clear decision. Do you want to adopt this law or belief for yourself? This is a time for commitment. If you like the law, it is clear to you. If you really want to make it a part of your own system, then decide to do so.

The final step is to begin the discipline necessary to make the new law your own. You really can change beliefs, but it will require disciplined activities for several weeks, several months, or even a year or more. It depends on where you are with your own belief system at the beginning of the discipline. You may already be ready to change because of a life experience, a trauma, or new material you have been reading or hearing. I make this point because some people think you can change a belief overnight—which simply is not true.

Before I share with you the specific disciplines used for accepting new laws and belief-changing, it might help to refer to a parable of Jesus. Matthew's Gospel tells the parable of the sower. Some seeds he planted fell on the hard path and never took root. Birds ate them before they could grow. Other seeds fell on shallow soil. They took root and sprung up immediately then withered away in the heat of day because they had very little roots. Still other seeds fell among thorns and weeds where they were choked out by what was already growing. Finally, some seed fell on good soil. They grew and produced much fruit.

This is a story more about soil than seed. It suggests that the soil, not the seed, determines growth. The ideas in this book are seeds. Your mind is the soil. If you are hard-headed, the seed will not grow. If you are shallow in your approach to learning, ideas will spring up rapidly and then wither away due to lack of commitment. If you refuse to weed out old prejudices, they will choke out the new beliefs. But if you open your mind and really commit to learning, the ideas can take root and produce a lot of good things in your life. The seeds are here. The soil is yours.

Five Steps

(1) *Decide to change.* This does not guarantee change. The only way you can know is by the follow-through. My youngest son, Russ, came back from a camp with this little riddle: "Three frogs were sitting on a log, and two of them decided to jump off. How many were left?" I responded, "One." "Nope." he grinned. "There would still be three. They only decided to jump. They never jumped." Deciding is not doing, but it is the first step.

(2) *Write the new law in your own words; commit it to memory.* Repeat it often. The number of times will differ from person to person. A general rule would be to repeat the new belief at least twelve times a day for at least a month. It should then become a habit.

(3) *Use your imagination.* Imagine or visualize some dramatic or humorous setting that will remind you of the new guideline or law. An example would be the belief that "I accept myself." This could be called the law of self-acceptance. In order to press the law into my mind, I will repeat it many times and then imagine that I see myself swinging from the limb of a tree with a monkey mask on, eating a banana, singing, "I accept myself as I am. I accept myself as I am." Every time I see a monkey, I will remember that I am learning to accept myself as I am. I expect I will remember it at other times as well. If this example does not appeal to you, do not despair; there will be others to follow.

(4) *Take the original thought and look for new ways to state it.* In other words, paraphrase the belief for yourself. You may find some old sayings or mottos that sum up the new belief. At the end of each

chapter I remind you to write, memorize, and repeat. I also list some suggested sayings.

(5) *Teach the new belief to someone else.* We learn by teaching. Try to convince as many people as you can that this new belief is a healthy one and would be helpful for them. I repeat these methods in many different ways throughout this book. You will learn by repetition.

CHAPTER 5

Perseverance

REMEMBER HOW TO EAT AN ELEPHANT? ONE BITE AT A TIME. THAT IS an excellent clue as to how we can make it through the pressures of life. We make it through one step at a time. Life is lived in increments. We seldom experience anything all at once.

Keep On Walking

How do we get through the educational system? One day, one book, one class, one paper, one problem at a time. When a child looks at the school system, it can be an overwhelming sight. Only when the child begins to take steps, one at a time, does he or she realize that it is not as big as it seems.

I was in the first grade. I had just learned to read the word "girl." Proud of my accomplishment, I got on the school bus and made my way back to sit by a friend's uncle Joe. Joe was a fifth grader. I sat down and grinned as I opened my "reader" and showed Joe the word "girl."

Joe was not a sensitive boy. Few fifth graders are. He opened his book and pointed to a word that looked like a foreign language to me. He beamed, "Handkerchief." I just knew I would never learn to read words as big as that. I did! I did it like I have had to do everything else in my life. I learned one word at a time. Even when it seems too hard to go on, we can't give up. We have to keep on walking, keep on learning one word at a time.

The Example of Athletes

Decathlon athletes are the epitome of perseverance. Most of us have seen the picture of decathlon participants, exhausted but struggling to finish an event. Their creed seems to be, "Ask not for victory; ask for courage. For if you can endure, you bring honor to us all. Even more, you bring honor to yourself."

In 1982, for 7 hours, Julie Moss led the competition in the Triathlon (a grueling test of endurance consisting of a 2.4-mile ocean swim, a 112-mile bicycle ride, and a 26.2-mile marathon). She collapsed just 50 feet from the finish line, but crawled across it to take second place. She later said, "I don't care what people thought. I wanted to finish that race."

We do not repeat the stories of people who fall near the finish line and just lie there. We tell of those who crawl to the finish. Life's battles don't always go to the strongest or fastest, but to those who continue the fight.

An Early Lesson

I was a freshman in high school and on the varsity track team. I was the smallest boy on the team and a miler! When we got ready to run the mile race in the county track meet, I was joined in the race by a sophomore, Hugh. In those days we drew little "pills" with numbers on them from a little black leather bottle. The lane in which we began the race was determined by the number we drew. The lowest number got the preferred inside position. I drew a 2. Hugh drew a 16. I believed Hugh had a better chance of winning for our team than I did, so I secretly switched "pills" with him. He thanked me and lined up on the inside of the track. I was on the outside and behind the other runners. Hugh dropped out of the race. He was the only person I beat, but I finished the race. I felt good about finishing the race.

It must have been my father who ground it into my head. Always finish what you start. Don't be a quitter. That lesson has dragged me across finish lines and through graduate programs. I will not quit, at least not as long as it is in my power to continue. The same principle that motivates us to finish races, games, and college courses motivates us to keep going through the times of pressure in life.

A Biblical Teaching

Jesus said, "No one who puts a hand to the plow and looks back is fit for the kingdom of God" (Luke 9:62). I don't know many people today who have ever put their hands on a plow, but a lot understand the principle. They know what it means to turn back or quit.

Near the end of his life, the apostle Paul said, "I have finished the race; I have kept the faith" (2 Tim 4:7). When he was on trial for his life, Paul told King Agrippa, "I was not disobedient to the heavenly vision" (Acts 26:19). He continued to pursue his dreams.

Life Is Seldom Easy

There are pains, problems, losses, sickness, and death. To expect life to be easy is to set one's self up for disappointment. Life is difficult. Once we realize this, we will be more likely to develop the courage to keep going. All great leaders have learned this lesson. Each of us must express it in our own way.

"A man in earnest finds means,
or if he cannot find means, he creates them." (Channing)
"The best way out is always through." (Robert Frost)
"Consider the postage stamp, my son. It secures success through its ability
to stick to one thing until it gets there." (Josh Billings)
"It ain't over till it's over." (Yogi Berra)

This is my belief: "I will keep on going as long as I have the strength to keep on going. I will face life by putting one foot in front of the other." During my lifetime I probably have said that to myself, in one form or another, thousands of times. I face the pressure with a deep belief that I will walk through it somehow, believing I can put one foot in front of the other.

Think of ways to say it to yourself. You will face many difficult days. Some days you will be wise to rest for a while, but never with the intention of just giving up on life. Repeat it to yourself in any way you can. I will share with you some of the ways I say it to myself.

I will not quit.
I will put one foot in front of the other until I make it through.
I am not a quitter.
I may not win, but I will finish the competition.

35

These words are written not only to fire people up to play a game, but with a belief that sometimes in life the only thing we can do is keep on walking. There are times when we walk through the fire, the tears, the pain, the fear. All we can do some of those days is just keep on walking.

Tough Times Will Come

I have described the law of perseverance in this brief chapter. I hope you will decide to adopt this law for yourself. Perhaps you will be helped to make the decision when I remind you of situations in which people have had to apply the principle.

- Don lost his wife and son in one accident. He walked on.
- Lee and Betty lost their youngest daughter in an accident. They walked on in faith.
- Alonzo and Retta lost their only grandchildren in an accident. They walked on by faith.

Even as I was writing this chapter, I received a telephone call from a friend who had lost his twelve-year-old grandson in an accident caused by a drunk driver. I marvel at his courage and grace. He is not bitter; he is resolute. He hurts, but he will keep on going by relying on God and walking through his tears. He is in the midst of deep pain.

Certainly there are thousands and thousands of people who moan and groan about minor pains, people who cry because it is too hot or too cold today, people who stay in bed when they have a sprained ankle, people who limp for weeks after the pain in their foot is gone simply because they want sympathy. That is one way to live, but to me it's not living. I want to develop more and more courage to walk on when the fires are blazing. I want to be able to walk through Gethsemene and pray with total conviction, "Father, if it is possible, let this cup pass from me. Nevertheless, let your will be done in my life." I want to develop the ability to say those words with peace and joy in my heart.

Thousands of people have developed the courage to walk on through the fire when they were diagnosed with cancer, faced the loss of a loved one, lost all of their material possessions, or faced the end of their own lives. We can do that too.

Don't Borrow Trouble

What I have been describing are situations where actual loss has occurred, but sometimes we feel tremendous pressure from things that have not happened and never do happen. Certainly there have been times when people have lived with the fear that something was going to happen and had stress and grief in anticipation. Some use this "worse case scenario" as a means of coping.

Mark Littell, a former Major League pitcher, told me that when he entered a difficult situation in a game, he would imagine the worse thing that could happen. When he imagined, for instance, that the hitter hit a home run, he could then relax.

I seldom use that kind of thinking, but it works for some people. I just don't like to worry too much in advance. "I've crossed that bridge a thousand times and never come to it yet." Don't borrow trouble. I may not have a job tomorrow, but I am working today. A focus on the present enables us to keep on walking through our fears.

Accept the Unexplained

Of course, tough times beyond our control and explanation will come. The Old Testament prophet Jeremiah complained about how hard life was for him. He was told that he had only run against footmen and would someday have to run against horses. He had just been wading in shallow streams but would someday have to face the swollen flood waters of the Jordan River.

There will come some hard times in every life—the loss of a marriage, a child, a job, a home, or a parent. There will be personal failures. There will be plenty of times to fear. There will be times when you know life is not fair. In those times, only a deep belief that we can keep going by putting together step after step after step will see us through.

It is important to put into your belief system the belief that there doesn't have to be an explanation to every circumstance. There doesn't have to be an obvious meaning in everything. Sometimes we have to blindly and painfully keep walking through the fires. That requires courage, courage grounded in the belief that we have the power within us to keep on walking.

Use Your Imagination

Certainly imagination is a powerful discipline we have too often left in our childhood. Experiment with your ability to imagine. Imagine yourself facing a very difficult situation. For example, you might imagine that your boss has just handed you a letter of dismissal. In your mind's eye, you know you are devastated. But in your imagination, you see yourself take the letter, fold it, put it into your pocket or purse, and with head held high, you walk out with the knowledge that this is one of those times when you just have to keep on walking.

Some of us begin to imagine worrisome situations when we lie down to sleep. Often our worries keep us awake. We can use those times to imagine bad things happening, but add to that image the picture of ourselves heroically walking through those times.

We often use our imaginations for worry and negative thoughts. Why not use them for empowerment? Prepare for the tough times with mental rehearsal. Prepare for the tough times by building a strong belief system. "I can make it, no matter what happens. I will just keep on putting one foot in front of the other."

Practice It and Teach It

Don't stop walking. Keep on keeping on! Persevere! If you decide to make this principle a part of your own belief system, you will need to follow through with the disciplines necessary to firmly implant the law in your own mind. The disciplines for changing your mind and accepting a new belief begin with repetition.

Repeat the law to yourself. "I will keep on walking. I have the courage to persevere. I will put one foot in front of the other. I can make it through the tough times by just continuing to move forward."

Many people find it helpful to quote favorite Bible passages to help them persevere in times of affliction. "I can do all things through him [Christ] who strengthens me" (Phil 4:13) Civil rights leaders made great use of songs to empower themselves and their followers during difficult times. "We shall overcome someday" became a theme that added to the courage needed to keep walking through the fires.

Sing it, repeat Bible passages, paraphrase it, or just repeat it. Say it so often that it will become a part of your deepest beliefs. "I have the courage to keep on walking."

Strengthen your beliefs by sharing them with others. Talk to friends, children, coworkers, students, teammates, or other family members about how important it is in your life to learn to walk on even in the difficult times. Our sharing with others will not only strengthen us, it will also help them to learn and prepare for the pressures of life.

When I walk through the fires of life, I will keep on walking. There is no place in life to just park until we die. Life is movement. Let's keep on walking. I will expect the best, prepare for the worst, and, by the grace of God, take whatever comes and keep on walking!

CHAPTER 6
Patience

THERE IS NO WISDOM IN DENYING PRESENT PAIN AND TROUBLE. THEY *do* exist. But they are made more bearable by knowing they will end, thus enabling us to develop an attitude of patience.

Patience is not limited to helping us cope with pain. It is also a part of being able to wait for good things. It permits the wines of life to fully ferment before we drink them. The recognition that we can continue to live in the now while waiting for future fulfillment is a mark of wisdom (Prov 19:11).

Patience can be paraphrased as "I can wait." "I can wait for this to pass." "I can wait for fulfillment" (for example, a car, a new home, sexual pleasure). The opposite of "I can wait" is "I just can't wait," which is an immature or almost infantile mentality. It leads to unwanted pregnancies, bankruptcy, misguided relationships, dropping out of school, and so on.

People who can't wait to feel good through healthy means will attempt to rush the process through the use of mind-altering drugs/alcohol. People who can't wait for pain to pass often just give up on living. There may come a time when the pain of going on is greater than the reward of living. At that point, we commit those persons to God and trust they will be at peace. When we struggle with pain, it is helpful to remember that the time will pass and we can make it.

The "I Can Wait" Lady

I got off a plane at Hilton Head Airport in South Carolina. There were several taxis waiting outside the small terminal. One of the taxis was driven by a small woman who appeared to be about sixty years old. She walked up to me, smiled, and said, "You looking for a good taxi?" She emphasized the word "good." I said I was in need of taxi service. She opened the door of a sleek, relatively new Cadillac.

In the course of my ride to my hotel, I got acquainted with Mary. She had just started her cab business. She called it the "Always Available Taxi Service." Mary explained that she had just moved south from New York City. She spoke with enthusiasm and some feistiness. I liked her. I asked if the taxi service was not a tough business for her to break into. She acknowledged that it was, but quickly added, "But I have a philosophy."

There was no need to ask what the philosophy was. She was eager to tell me. "First, I will give extra services to my customers. I stop and let them pick up needed supplies from convenience stores and offer to come back and pick them up if they need to go shopping." Part of the "extra" service was to keep her cab clean (it was clean) and to give special attention to each customer. Her idea was to give better service and get more customers, which is not a novel idea in business, but it is somewhat novel to practice it.

The second part of her philosophy was this: "I know I am going to make it, because I can wait. I ain't in no hurry. I'm not going anywhere, and I'll get return business. If you come back again, will you call me?" I looked at the card she had given me and nodded, "Yes, I'll call you." I will, and she will wait.

A Lesson from the Caribbean

If you want a "quick" course in patience (Most of us do. We want patience, and we want it right now!), spend some time in the Caribbean Islands. You will find a lot of relaxed people there. I suppose the hot weather makes rushing impractical. Patience is a coping skill that should be on the endangered species list, but it is alive and well in Puerto Rico.

I arrived in San Juan and got to my hotel just an hour and a half before a big heavyweight title fight. I wanted very much to see the fight and hoped there would be time for dinner before the fight began. My host assured me that the maitre d' would get us in and out in plenty of time for us to watch the fight. We entered the restaurant and explained our situation. Following is my memory of the events from that point throughout the rest of the evening.

The maitre d' said, "No problem." He then walked away and did not return for almost fifteen minutes. Then we were escorted to a table toward the rear of the restaurant. About five minutes later, we were explaining our plight to a waiter who smiled knowingly and assured us, "No problem."

It was at least another ten minutes when he returned with the menu. Again, my friend explained our need to hurry and told the waiter that we were ready to order right then. He nodded and left to get water for us. He returned in about five minutes with water, and we ordered our food.

Salads were served in a little less than twenty minutes. My host, Ted, explained that we needed to get our main course before we finished our salads, and this, of course, was "no problem." Ted noticed the time was late, so he called the waiter over and informed him that we would not be able to wait for our food. We needed to get the bill, which was "no problem." We were walking out of the restaurant ten minutes past time for the fight to begin, and I realized finally that "no problem" meant "no problem to them."

Ted and I hurried to a bar where we could watch the big screen television. We were frustrated but didn't know each other well enough to really express our feelings. He apologized for our being late. I almost said, "No problem." I didn't. I just smiled and lied that it was alright. Guess what? The fight did not begin for two hours. I became so bored with the preliminaries that I decided to go to my room and watch a small screen. I do not remember watching the fight, but I must have because it was so important that I had hurried to see it.

In retrospect (my hindsight is 20/20), I realize I often hurry, hurry—only to find it is not necessary. Learn the lesson of patience. The ability to wait can help us to relax. When people can't wait, they waste a lot of time pushing ropes uphill and fanning embers into forest fires. We sometimes call this "Type A" behavior.

Things Do Change

I work for a company that has gone through major changes in personnel in the last five years. At one time, at least fifty jobs were eliminated in a certain department. Some of the people who held those jobs moved on to other companies. Some accepted other jobs in the same company. About twenty-five people were just out of work. In less than six months, "the powers that be" decided that they really needed more people in the very same department. In fact, they needed an additional twenty people. The result was bringing people back and even hiring new people.

Who can explain it? The point is, often things change if we just have the patience to wait. Sometimes they change; sometimes they don't. But patience is almost always a positive way to cope.

A Biblical Concept

Patience is called a "fruit of the spirit" (Gal 5:22). Christians are to be "clothed with patience" (Col 3:12). According to the book of James, patience brings about perseverance, which leads to perfection. Patience is an attribute of love (1 Cor 13:4). We are patient with the people we love.

At Least Slow Down

My friend, "Woody," is a slow-talking, soft-spoken gentleman. He says, "You can have just about anything you want if you are willing to wait for it, but no one can have everything he wants." We have to make choices and then be willing to exercise patience.

The concept is important simply because there are so many things in life that just will not be rushed. Acorns refuse to grow into oak trees overnight. Babies take their time about being born. Snails move slowly. And most Southerners talk slowly, but they all seem to get where they are going eventually.

Those of us who took time to read the story of the tortoise and the hare remember the virtue of perseverance and patience. The hare was so busy being busy and distracted, he lost the race.

I started dreaming of a Ph.D. when I was twenty-three years old. I plugged along until I earned it at the age of forty-nine. I just kept telling myself that the time would pass whether or not I was working on the degree. I'm glad I had the patient endurance to finish it.

Impatience breeds anxiety and destroys coping skills. Recent studies suggest that even our immune systems are retarded by anxiety. Anxious, impatient people are more likely to become ill than their more relaxed, patient counterparts.

An Outgrowth of Reality

I cannot change reality, so I either face it or live in denial. My son, Bill, told me that facing reality is "2 x 2" thinking. Two times two is four. It was four yesterday. It will be four tomorrow. It is four today. Normal people look at the equation and say, "Yes, that is four." Neurotic people look at the equation and say, "Yes, that is four, but I wish it was five. Maybe it will be five if I look at it a little harder." Two times two is four. Accept it. This is a rough translation of the serenity prayer. I can't change it, so I will accept it.

Imagine traffic lined up for three miles ahead of you. There are two lines of cars between you and the exit lane. No one is moving. Look around. You see people pounding their steering wheels. Some get out of their cars and try to see the end of the line. Some fellow even honks his horn—as if that will move three miles of traffic. Look over to the side and see a man sitting there listening to his radio, smiling and saying, "Well, two times two is four. I wish it wasn't, but it is. Here I sit, so I might as well make the most of it." I am that man. I haven't always been, but I am now.

I see a lot of people who have been diagnosed with catastrophic diseases. I try to help them apply the same logic to disease as to traffic. "I have the disease. I wish I didn't, but I do." Only when we accept the fact of disease can we effectively fight it. Only then can we develop the patience to cope.

An Attitude Based in Our Belief

You can grow in patience and the ability to cope with the pressures of life if you work on your belief system. Begin to repeat the belief to yourself in your own words. Write it. Record it. Teach it to others.

I am patient.
I can wait.
Time will pass, so I will make the most of now.
I don't sweat the small stuff, and it's all small stuff.
Few things are worth dying for.
This won't matter fifty years from now.
I am patient.

Think of as many ways as you can to verbalize the law. Say it until you grind it into your belief system. Patience is better than pride (Eccl 7:8). Life is sometimes hard, but it will end. Be patient. It will help you to walk through the fires of life.

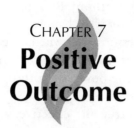

CHAPTER 7

Positive Outcome

A LOT OF MISERY AND POOR HEALTH RESULT FROM EXPECTING THINGS to go wrong. This falls into the category of self-fulfilling prophecy. When walking through the fires of life, a mind full of negative expectations is like a tank of gasoline.

One friend of mine expected things to go so poorly for him that he claimed as his theme song, "Born to Lose." Poor old Max! About all he was good for was to be a bad example. He was a living example of "Murphy's Law." Do you have that trouble?

If you have found yourself believing that things just never seem to work out right for you, then you may need a *metanoia,* a change of mind. Consider this statement: By the grace of God, I can make it work for me. When I remember this, I worry a lot less about crashing and keep looking for landing lights. My life is made better by this belief. No matter how difficult the moment, it can be turned into something worthwhile. This is another way of saying, "Everything works together for good in my life."

All Things Work Together for Good

Will your life be made better by believing in positive outcomes? I believe it will. We can handle the pressures more effectively and feel better in general if we embrace this conviction. When people believe that nothing works for them, they are usually right. When people believe that everything works in their favor, they are usually right. The belief is valid, not because everything that happens is good, but because we have the power and ability to find good results or even to create positive results from whatever happens. The Bible verbalizes this concept in these words: "All things work together for good for those who love God, who are called according to his purpose" (Rom 8:28).

In *Unlimited Power,* Anthony Robbins states this as one of the "lies" of success: "No matter what happens, it works for me." He calls this a "lie" because it doesn't matter whether it is true or not. It is true for people who believe it. Even in the secular world the concept is helpful. When we add the power of faith to the belief, it becomes tremendously helpful.

When something is true and effective, you will find it in some form in the belief systems of most successful and healthy people. This belief of positive outcome will show up in various forms in the Bible, self-help books, and autobiographical material of successful people. I am not arguing that everything that happens is good. I am arguing that no matter what happens in our lives, we can choose to put a frame around it that will be positive and helpful. We can make things work for us.

Debate with yourself. Would you be happier and more excited about life if you believed it would work in your favor to take what is and make the most of it without complaining? I believe the answer is "Yes."

A Real-Life Example

It was not a good or positive thing when John, an active softball player, was diagnosed with ALS (Lou Gehrigs's disease). This deteriorating nerve condition debilitates the muscles alongside the spinal column. It was made less painful for John, however, because of his attitudes and choices. He chose to accept what he could not change and change what he could. While this is not a new concept, it is fresh every time someone like John applies it to life. John couldn't change the fact that he had the disease, so he changed his lifestyle. He said, "I couldn't play any longer, so I did something I could do. I became a coach."

When I spoke to John recently, the disease had progressed to the point that he was confined to a wheelchair. He smiled and said, "Well, I can't coach any longer, but I can be a fan." John is taking life by the throat and patiently enduring victoriously. He has the kind of courage that enables him to make things work for him. Others with the same condition have become depressed, withdrawn, bitter, or even suicidal. What makes the difference?

The difference is in the attitude, the belief systems. John finds a way to make the most of life. He believes in one of our basic rights. He has a right to give meaning and purpose to his own life. He can choose to adjust to circumstances. John is making sure, as fully as he can, that everything works for him. He believes it. He acts as if it is true. For him, it is true.

An Early Lesson

I learned to reframe experiences into positives and make them work for me when I was still a child. In our school lunchroom there was a table for those of us who could not afford to pay even nominal fees for daily lunches. (In those days, there really were no free lunches). At our table we were each given a carton of lukewarm milk to go with the lunches we had brought from home.

I remember one day looking at the face of a friend. He was drooling over the lunches others were eating in the cafeteria while fingering his milk carton. I really felt his pain (our pain) of poverty. The light-bulb flashed in my head, an idea! I said to him, "Man, I'm glad we don't have to eat that lunchroom food. I don't like light bread. I love these home-cooked biscuits." We grinned at each other and ate our biscuits. We had reframed our situation and made it work for us.

A Choice

While serving as pastor of the Christ Memorial Baptist Church in St. Louis County, I bought a 500 SE Mercedes. It was something I had dreamed of for more than thirty years. I drove that lapis blue beauty to a church camp at the Lake of the Ozarks.

I was greeted there by a man who was one of those "good" people from whom I have often prayed for deliverance. You may know the type. They have a way of looking down at you. They speak with rounded tones, and their heads often snap back when they say "God." He asked me if the car was mine. I confirmed it was. His head snapped back as he said, "God would not be pleased with a minister driving that kind of car." I supposed it would have been all right for a layperson, but not a minister.

I received inspiration at that moment. I smiled and reframed his comment to work for me. I said, "You are absolutely right. I just cannot afford the kind of car God wants me to drive." His expression changed. He said nothing as he walked away. I don't remember him smiling, but I thought it was amusing. Because of my deep belief that everything works for me, I was able to reframe his comment into one that worked for me. I enjoyed that. In fact, I am still enjoying it. Amazing how belief and attitude can take a potentially difficult situation and transform it into a happy one!

If we can accept the truth that all things can work for us, we can even reframe our memories into more positive experiences. We cannot change our history, but we have the right to interpret it for ourselves. We have all heard people talk about the poverty in their past, saying, "It was the best thing that could have happened to us. We grew closer than ever and really learned to appreciate what we have." Even our poverty can be made to work for us!

We make choices about the frames we put around our lives. We can whine about being so poor that "we just didn't have the chance that others did." Bad things happen to us because we are poor, women, men, black, white, uneducated, or socially disadvantaged. But we can take those same things and turn them into things that work for us. We will be more energized, happier, and healthier if we believe that things work for us.

Some Old Stories

There are literally hundreds of stories in motivational books and on tapes about people who have turned tragedy into triumph, loss into gain, grief into joy, and defeat into victory.

The apostle Paul was in prison when he wrote the Epistles (letters) that now form the heart of Christian theology. He wrote beautiful inspirational material such as the book of Philippians, which tells of patient, victorious courage that grew out of dealing with the pressures of life. Paul made the situation work for him.

John Bunyan was also in prison. He could have wilted away in self-pity. Rather he chose to make the most of his circumstance. He let the situation work for him. He wrote the book *Pilgrim's Progress* from his prison cell.

I love the story about the general whose troops were completely surrounded by the enemy. He is reported to have said, "Men, never before has an army had a chance to attack in all directions." It is often a matter of interpretation. It is always a matter of choice and attitude.

Out of the Job Trap

A salesman was in my office to talk about his sense of failure. He was making a lot of money, but he still was unhappy. He had taken the job he presently held because his father wanted him to. Jim's father died two years ago. Since then, Jim has had an increasing dissatisfaction with his work. He no longer has to please his father, but is now afraid to change. He might not be able to make it in a new situation.

This story is repeated in one form or another by hundreds of people. I hear it often. Many people would like to change professions but are simply afraid to take the step. Yet, those same people are terribly shaken by the thought of a cutback in personnel. Frequently, a person who is forced out of a job is suddenly free from the old job trap and has an opportunity to do something for which he or she is much better suited.

If you are facing the loss of a job because of re-engineering, you might make it work for you by taking the opportunity to move into something better for you. That doesn't always happen, but it never happens to the people who do not expect it to happen. Look for the opportunity. Make it happen for you.

Optimism: The Child of Adversity

It fascinates me to see how consistently survivors, winners, and generally successful people practice the freedom to reframe or reinterpret their experiences in the light of their belief that anything can and will work for them. Adversity seems to be a necessary teacher of optimism. I agree with those who note that some of our best writing is done when we hurt the most.

The choice is ours. We learn to sing happy songs when we are walking through the gutter of pain and poverty. Songs of happiness sung in the fair weather seem to have less depth than those melodies that penetrate the dark corridors of human pain. Maybe we only learn to sing of hope when we walk in the valleys, and maybe only fellow valley-walkers can grasp the meaning of our songs. Hope is wrapped in the tears of despair, which prompted my following piece of poetry.

Prism of Tears

I cannot mature in love
Without the passing of years,
And I see God most clearly
Through the prism of my tears.
Yes, through the prism,
Through the prism of my tears,
I see God most clearly
Through the prism of my tears.

I learned to see my loss
As a chance for me to gain.
I even understand it
When my sky is clouded with pain.
Then through the prism,
Through the prism of my tears,
I see God most clearly
Through the prism of my tears.

The unhappy and frequently unhealthy fatalist says of life, "The bad things that happen are simply the will of God." Such people then live as if God is responsible for whatever happens in life. Others, who are happier and healthier, say, "I will make it work for me."

Four Disciplines

(1) Do you want to make this belief a part of your life? If you do, then take the time right now to write beneath this paragraph, *"I have decided to accept the conviction that everything works for me."* Sign your name and date it. Beliefs are decisions! Begin today to act as if everything in life works for you. Filter your experiences through that belief. Reframe situations and even history to make them work for you.

You have already taken the first step if you have decided to adopt this belief into your system or to reaffirm it as part of your system of thinking. Remember, deciding is not doing. Before doing anything else, at least take step two. It will be a way of riveting down the decision in your life. Just as a person can choose to believe in God, one can choose to adopt healthy beliefs.

(2) *Write the belief, either as I have written it—"Everything works together for good in my life"—or in your paraphrase.* Repeat it to yourself at least twelve times slowly right now. You can't repeat healthy thoughts too often. Repetition is a tool used by Christians through the years. By repetition we memorize Scripture and put it into our belief systems. Many theologians believe that Jesus had done that with the 22nd Psalm. It was so much a part of his mind that when he was hurting and dying on the cross, he repeated portions of the passage.

(3) *Use your imagination to see yourself applying this belief in a difficult situation.* An example would be to imagine that you just lost your job. You could imagine yourself talking to a friend and saying, "I wonder what wonderful thing is going to come out of this experience for me. I know something good will, because everything works together to bring something good in my life."

(4) Another way of implementing the second step is to *paraphrase the belief.* It is another way of repeating the idea. Here are some possible paraphrases:

Everything works for me.
I always land on my feet.
I come out smelling like a rose.
All of my clouds have silver linings.
All things work for good to those who believe in God.
Things just have a way of working out.
I make lemonade from the lemons in my life.

Practice It and Teach It

When you imagine yourself acting on this belief, how do you feel? When I think of things working out for me, I feel good inside. Think about how good you will feel the next time something appears to be bad in your life and you employ *metanoia* and turn the whole experience into something useful.

Record your voice on an audiotape repeating this concept to yourself. Make yourself conscious of the belief so that every time you see it in a book, newspaper article, or magazine, it will jump out at you. Find ways to repeat it. Remember, we learn from repetition.

The first opportunity you have, teach the new belief to someone. Perhaps you can call a friend and talk to him/her about it. Ask what your friend's belief is. Tell the person how this belief can be used to transform bad into good or at least can move in the direction of making it better.

Conclusion

Ultimately, the belief and action must be in agreement in order to empower life. If I believe that everything works for me and act as if this is true, then my life is permeated with a positive atmosphere.

You have put one more stone in the foundation of your deepest foundation for living. One by one, put the thoughts, ideas, or beliefs into your system so that you will live a happier and healthier life. "As you think, so you are."

Pressures will come. We will walk through the fires. The belief that everything can have a positive outcome has helped me to walk through my trials. This is a vital law for fire walkers. As long as I believe in the redeeming power of God to work good from all my circumstances, I believe I will always land on my feet! Change your beliefs; change your life!

CHAPTER 8
Contentment

ONE OF THE MOST POWERFUL CONCEPTS WE'LL EVER DISCOVER IS THE idea that we can be content with what we have and where we are. Not many people believe this. Contentment is hard to sell to Americans because it is often viewed as weakness. When fully understood, it is a wonderful coping tool.

"Content" comes from the Greek word *arkeo,* which means "to be possessed of unfailing strength, to be strong, to suffice, to be enough to ward off any danger." It implies the strength to accept and deal effectively with any circumstance and is grounded in the concept of God's grace. Because God's grace is sufficient, we can handle any situation (2 Cor 12:9).

"Contentment" comes from a combination of two Greek words: *autos,* which is the personal possessive "our," and *arkeo.* The combination *autarkas* implies sufficiency in one's self. It is a strength that is independent of external circumstances. This was Paul's word in Phillipians 4:7-13. He was saying that because of Christ's power within him, he had learned to find the strength within to accept all circumstances with equal serenity.

According to the Greek definition, we can identify contentment not as weakness, but as a great strength. It is an attitude expressed internally as, "I have nothing to prove." It grows out of personal security and maturity. It is expressed as a deep sense of confidence that we can handle whatever comes.

If we really embrace this concept, we will be free of most stress and can experience great peace. If you want to raise the level of your joy in life, reduce your conflict, and strengthen your coping skills, then begin today to take what is and make the most of it without complaining. An example might be someone in a troubled marriage. When he or she decides to take what is, that person becomes content and is free to work to make the relationship as good as possible. Ultimate success of the marriage is not guaranteed, but it certainly gives it a better chance.

A Hard Concept to Accept

> To proud Americans, contentment is something to be enjoyed between birth and kindergarten . . . retirement and the rest home . . . or among those who have no ambition.
>
> Charles Swindoll
> *The Quest for Character*

We are quick to criticize those who are content. Perhaps we envy them, or perhaps we have bought into the suggestion that the only way to live is to strive each day for more and better.

How many of our friends have turned down a promotion because they were happy with their present work? They had no desire to be a foreman, supervisor, or manager. How un-American!! Who made the rule that a young man who is gifted with mechanical skills should not pursue a vocational or trade school education rather than attend a fine arts college? What is wrong with a competent teacher wanting to stay in the classroom rather than take an administrative job?

Nothing is wrong with those decisions. It is certainly alright to be happy where you are. Perhaps the important issue is motivation. When we are motivated out of fear, it is probably not good. But if we are motivated out of a strong sense of security (contentment), there is nothing wrong with desiring to stay where we are. If you are happy with where you are, then do not yield to the pressure to change just for the sake of change. As Bob Biehl said in his book, *Stop Setting Goals,* "Do not try to be someone you are not. It will cause you great stress and deep frustration" The fact is, many people are so afraid of what others will think that they are afraid not to move upward. After all, it is the American way.

A Biblical Concept

"If we have food and clothing . . . be content" (1 Tim 6:8). "Keep your lives free from the love of money, and be content with what you have" (Heb 13:5). The apostle Paul said he had learned the secret of being content no matter what his outward circumstances (Phil 4:4-13). The book of James tells us that we war and fight with one another because we want to consume things for ourselves (4:1-3).

A Learned Response

We don't begin with a deep sense of contentment. We have to learn it. My happiness and security never reside in external circumstances. Think of it. What is secure in this world? Life? Of course not. We can lose life in the flash of an eye. Job? People who think security and happiness can be found in a job have not heard of downsizing or re-engineering. They have not met the new breed of greed that comes in the form of hired guns to come into a company and get rid of as many employees as possible without shutting down the business. Companies close, move, go bankrupt, or just "let people go." Don't think for one minute that you can find security or happiness in a job.

Some of us have looked in relationships. There is no perfect or permanent relationship. If you do not lose a relationship through separation by choice, you will someday lose it to death. I am not trying to be negative, just realistic. There is no lasting happiness or security in material things. Material things will all pass away. Contentment must come from inside. It is a decision that we will take what is and make the most of it without griping.

An Internal Commitment

Internal contentment removes false distinctions. It produces a sense of equality. We cannot judge the value or strength of someone by their desire to move up in society or stay where they are. Strip away our name brand clothes, take away our luxury automobiles, and stand us nude in a mob. We are all in this together. The knowledge that we have enormous worth and value helps us to accept one another as equals and experience freedom from phony distinctions.

Commitment to the here and now is at the base of contentment. This is all I have, so I might as well make the most of it. My father used to say, "All you can do is all you can do." When you do all you can do, there is no need to worry and fret. I paraphrase this idea when dealing with any pressure in life. I want to be realistic. All I have is all

I have, and what I have right now is what I have right now. I may wish it otherwise, but it is what is. The only sane thing to do is accept what exists and start working with it.

I am most content and function with greater internal strength when I have done the things I really respect. When I know something is good for me to do, I am restless until I do it. If I need to make a visit, I feel better internally when I make the visit. Contentment grows out of the courage to go ahead and do the things we believe are best for us to do.

How Much Is Enough?

What is at the source of marital fights? Dissatisfaction. We are not getting what we want or enough of what we want, so we fight. What is the cause for most divorces? We want someone else's wife or husband. We are always looking over fences to see what is more desirable. We would usually be better off weeding our own gardens than planting new ones. Contentment comes when we stop looking at greener grass in the other yard and start greening our own, feeling content with what we have.

When Henry Ford was asked "How much is enough?" he responded, "Enough is always one dollar more than you have." When will we have enough? Enough money, property, things? For most people, that time will never come.

I really respected my father and learned a lot of valuable things from him. He did, however, have a weak spot. He had grown up during the Depression and was always concerned that he might not have enough money to get by during his retirement years. He once said to me, "If I had enough money to make it for ten more years, I'd start traveling and living it up." I said, "You do have enough for ten more years." Dad responded, "Yea, but what if I live eleven?" He didn't. He died of a stroke just a little over a year later.

When will we have enough to be content? When we decide that what we have is enough.

Help with Pressures

I can never deal effectively with any situation until I honestly accept it as a reality in my life. Denial has never, to my knowledge, proven to be an effective stance for coping with the pressures of life. Powerful coping is simply a matter of applying the serenity prayer to life. We have to learn to change the situations we can change, accept the situations we cannot change, and pray for the wisdom to know the difference.

When I am confronted with a pressure in life, I want to learn to ask, "What can I do about this situation?" If the answer is "Nothing," I want to learn to ask, "Then what can I do?" This question leads me to seek an answer that will move me back into the things I can control.

There are certainly times when I can do nothing to change a situation. Those are the times when I want to resolve to accept what is and make the most of it. That is possible only when I have a deep sense of internal strength (contentment) about myself. Contentment is an inside job.

Internalize the Law

Imagine yourself in a situation where you would have been disturbed or distressed. You are very calm and honestly feel a deep sense of contentment. You have asked yourself if there is anything you can do but have found nothing. You have then said to yourself, "I can take what is and make the most of it. I am not going to waste my energy complaining about this."

If you want to press this belief into your own system of beliefs, then repeat it, write it, imagine it is true, teach the concept to others. You might even want to make a tape of yourself describing contentment and repeating some of the ways you say it to yourself. Repeat to yourself:

I am learning to be content with whatever my circumstances.
I take what is and make the most of it without complaining.
I am a contented person, a person who knows he has the power
within to overcome in any and all circumstances.

We can become more content by embracing the principles described here, but we will have to work at it. Remember, our beliefs and behaviors were not developed overnight; they will not be changed overnight. I sincerely hope you can learn to apply this principle to your life. It will ease your stress. For now I am content!

CHAPTER 9
Responsibility

WHEN PRESSURES COME INTO OUR LIVES, WE ARE TEMPTED TO RUN away. If we cannot literally run, we may try to at least hide from the responsibility for dealing with the situation—which is a self-defeating behavior. Almost every problem we face is reduced in power when we stand face to face with it and accept the responsibility for finding a solution.

> *"The buck stops here."* (Harry Truman)
> *"You reap what you sow."* (the Bible)
> *"Every tub has to sit on its own bottom."* (Ma Little)

I earlier referred to Charles Sykes' book, *A Nation of Victims*. It points out the trend in this country to excuse our problem behaviors. We have learned to blame others for our problems, our failures at work or at home, even our crimes. Sykes tells the story of a school employee who showed up for work late every day. The employee was warned, put on probation, and ultimately fired. After being fired, the worker hired a psychiatrist and a lawyer. (Although we need these two professions, we do not need those who use their positions to create more work for themselves.) It was determined that this person was suffering from "chronic lateness syndrome." One of my friends calls this the dreaded "CLS." The employee won the court battle and had to be reinstated.

Some people may think this story is funny; it is frightening to me. We are creating a society where people do not want to take responsibility for their own behavior. Chronic lateness is a result of not setting a clock for an early-enough hour. If someone can get up and be at work fifteen minutes late, they can get there on time. It is not a sickness. It is a result of laziness or lack of discipline.

We are so afraid of wounding someone's self-esteem that we have bent over backwards to absolve people of responsibility. We have permitted the pendulum to swing too far. We are creating monsters. There was a time when it was "American" to accept responsibility. That characteristic has faded out of the picture. I, for one, am sick and tired of absolving everyone of personal responsibility. We excuse murder, rape, and child abuse on the bases of "sickness." Fall in love with responsibility. It is a wonderful thing.

There are plenty of reasons now for us to grab an excuse and hide behind it. Look around and listen. "Well, it's not my fault." "I am not responsible." When manufacturing plants close down, management blames labor, and labor blames management. Then, both blame foreign imports. When was the last time you said or heard someone say, "I am responsible"?

Prerequisite for Leadership

President John F. Kennedy publicly acknowledged that the Bay of Pigs invasion in the early 1960s was a mistake. He said, "I am responsible." Some have suggested that as a result of his admission, Kennedy became accepted as a leader. The willingness to accept responsibility is a prerequisite for leadership.

Self-Esteem Developer

People almost always live in a manner that is consistent with their own self-esteem. We are basically what we believe we are in our deepest and strongest selves. Again, the Bible teaches that as we think inside ourselves, so we are. If we feel good about ourselves, it will show in our attitudes toward relationships, work, and play. Few fail to see the value of self-esteem, but we seldom have made the connection between esteem and a sense of responsibility.

Thomas Connellan reported studies on the core conditions for developing "self-starters." The studies indicate that, while firstborn children make up less than one third of the population, they make up an unusually high percentage of high achievers. For example, twenty-one of the first twenty-two astronauts were firstborn children. Almost two thirds of the people listed in "Who's Who in America" are firstborn children. The same percentage is found in the highest ranking students on college campuses.

I certainly doubt that firstborn children are any smarter than the secondborn, thirdborn, or any others. What then accounts for this difference in achievement level? At least one contributing factor is the fact that firstborn children are given more responsibility than their younger siblings. This is usually not by design. It just happens because parents assign responsibility to the oldest child in the family.

I was the oldest child in my family. When my parents left home to do errands, they left me in charge. I remember clearly them saying to me, "You are responsible for your brother and sisters, because you are the oldest." When we went to the movies, I was given the money and told to see that my sisters and brother got their tickets and some popcorn and a soda. I may have complained about the responsibility at times, but there certainly was a sense of pride at being left in charge. Though I didn't realize it at the time, it made me feel good about myself. Parents would be wise to delegate responsibility to all their children. It is one way of helping them build good self-esteem.

Employees who are not given responsibility often become inefficient and careless workers. I have heard this statement, "It doesn't make any difference what I do. I'm not important here anyway." If we want employees to have higher motivation, we must communicate to them their importance to the organization. One way to communicate significance is to assign important responsibilities to all workers and consistently emphasize that there are no unimportant jobs or people in the organization.

Ingredient for Successful Living

People who go through life blaming others for their circumstances will usually be far more unhappy than those who accept the responsibility for themselves. We have all heard the "if onlys" from people around us: "If only it had not been for my background, I would have . . ." "If only I had not been born black, I would have . . ." "If only my parents had not been so severe with me, I would have . . ." "If only I were not a woman, I would have . . ." The list goes on and on. Remember, when we blame others for our own life situations, we are at the same time reducing our own self-esteem.

Excuse making is the opposite of accepting responsibility. It sets us up for failure. It can be deadly. One mother mistakenly wrote a note for her son, "Billy was sick with a sore throat last night so he cannot participate in gym. Please execute him." The fact is, habitual excuse making can kill character.

Real-Life Examples

I played basketball in college with a young redhead from Louisiana. We made a road trip to southern Texas one weekend. It was his first such trip. Our coach gave us meal money each morning for the day's meals. "Red" thought it was money for breakfast, so he ate a tremendous breakfast and was without money for the rest of the day. At dinner he had only two thin dimes. Even when I went to college, twenty cents wouldn't buy much food.

Following the game that evening, several of us stopped in the hotel coffee shop for a snack. We all ordered while "Red" fingered his two dimes. When the waitress came to him, he ordered a glass of buttermilk and a package of crackers. He told us he could eat the crackers in the buttermilk and it would "bloat" enough to make him feel full. One of the players offered to lend him some money. I liked his response and have never forgotten it. "No, thanks. I made my own bed, and I aim to lie in it." He was responsible. I liked him. The last I heard of him he had become the superintendent of a school in his home state.

More recently, a St. Louis paper carried an article about W. Mitchell. Mitchell was involved in a motorcycle accident that resulted in burns on 65 percent of his body. He was given up for dead but survived. This man wisely invested the insurance money in, of all things, a wood burning stove business, which turned into a small fortune.

If that was the end of the story, it would be inspiring enough. It would certainly indicate that a man who could have excused himself from any kind of work accepted responsibility for himself and became very successful. But there is more to the story. Mitchell became a private pilot, and while flying with ice on the wings of his plane, he crashed. As a result, he became a paraplegic. That was excuse enough to quit again. He did not quit. From his wheelchair, he went into politics. He ran for attorney general of his state.

W. Mitchell refused to blame anyone. He didn't blame God, himself or others. He just took responsibility for his own life and moved forward. He refused to wallow in self-pity. He eloquently stated his reaction: "Before all this I could do about 10,000 things. Now there are about 1,000 things I cannot do. I can still do 9,000 things. I choose to focus on the 9,000 I can do and not the 1,000 I cannot do." He is more than a coping person. He is a victorious person who has demonstrated the courage sufficient to deal with any pressure.

Catalyst for Empowerment

As sure as excuse making weakens us, responsibility empowers us. Excuse making causes us to feel like victims. To be aware that we are in charge of ourselves has become the captain of our own destinies. This means I have the power of God in my life to enable me to be whatever God wants me to become. I am not a victim; I am a participant in my own life. Life does not happen to me; I happen to life. As long as I recognize this, I can manage my own life. Being responsible means I have the power to do something about my life.

> *I am responsible.*
> *I am responsible for my own emotions.*
> *I am responsible for my own behavior.*
> *I am responsible for my own results.*
> *I am responsible for my own diet.*
> *I am responsible for my own discipline.*
> *I am responsible for my own health program.*
> *I am responsible for my own beliefs.*
> *I am responsible for my own attitudes.*
> *I am responsible for my own habits.*
> *I am responsible for my own worship.*
> *I am responsible for my own study habits.*
> *I am responsible for my own work habits.*
> *I am responsible for my own life.*
> *I am responsible.*

I recently saw a campaign within a large manufacturing company called the "I Am 100% Responsible" campaign. The idea was to help each person to accept 100%-responsibility for his or her contribution to the success of the company. It is a quality program that seems to be working.

Some people find copping out more desirable than coping. They like being victims. These are the people who are generally not healthy and certainly not much fun to be around. Victims try to cope by saying, "I just can't help it. It isn't my fault." If your mind runs in that rut, you may be getting by in life. But is that how you want to live? Not me.

I used to complain about being too busy until one of my more honest friends asked me, "Who makes your schedule?" That question, coupled with McCays' suggestion that we can learn to smile and say "No" until our tongues bleed, has changed my life in a positive way. I like being in charge of my own decisions. I like steering my own ship. It is my choice.

Stop for a moment and make a list of the people you consider the healthiest, happiest, and perhaps most successful people you know. Are they excuse makers or people who assume responsibility for themselves? Think about it. Who can do something about the pressures in your life? You can, if you choose to be responsible.

Conclusion

Ezekiel 33 states a proverb about a time when people believed that if the parents ate sour grapes, the children's teeth were set on edge. In other words, the sins of the father were placed on the children. Ezekiel said that proverb was no longer to be quoted. Rather, the soul that sinned would die. It was his way of saying that we are responsible for our own actions.

I am responsible for myself. When will we start living as if that is true? Excuses are for losing and not for living. Be responsible. It is a law of coping. I can handle the pressures in my life. I am responsible!

Chapter 10
Integrity

STEPHEN COVEY SAYS THAT INTEGRITY IS ESSENTIAL TO PERSONAL productivity. You cannot maintain the energy necessary to be consistently productive in your personal life, your family life, or your work life unless you maintain integrity with yourself. There is tremendous power in knowing what is important to you and then living according to that value.

A couple of years ago, I spoke to a group of contractors in Dallas, Texas. Our topic was "values clarification." I seriously doubted the topic would be exciting to the group, but they were gracious enough to listen. The more we talked, the more interested they became. I discovered that these people were really concerned about values. They just were not open with each other about these ideas. I was reminded of the old adage about Baptists being the people who do not drink in front of each other. There are a lot of feelings and thoughts that we are not free to share with one another, but when one person shares them, often an avalanche of pent-up feelings follows.

That avalanche happened in Dallas. People who had not talked about their own real values for a long time were pouring out their feelings and experiencing a lot of positives as a result. We became close as a group almost instantly.

One fellow from Phoenix was especially moved by the experience. Frank, who was leading the conference, asked me to stop by the man's room. The door to George's room was slightly ajar. George was seated at the desk at the end of the room. He wore cowboy boots, a belt with a big buckle, and jeans. He was sitting there crying. Frank had no idea what the problem was, so he sort of pushed me into the room and closed the door behind me. I asked, "How are you doing?"

"Never better," he blubbered. "That session today on values helped me a lot. I knew I was right to focus on my family, but no one had ever come right out and said that was alright. I came to the room and called my wife. I told her I was going to cut back on the time I spend with work projects and spend more time with the family. She said that was what she needed to hear. She was really encouraged. Thanks for helping me to see that I can live by my own values."

Permission Not Required

We don't need permission from anyone to live according to our own values as long as those values do not interfere with the rights of others or hurt them. I am amazed that there is so much power in peer pressure or the pressure of opinion in general.

A few years ago I did a brief study with students in a local high school. I interviewed them at the beginning of the school year. I asked them what kind of grades they expected to get in an English course, what their parents expected them to get, and what their friends expected them to get. I was asking for their perceptions of the views of their parents and friends. Amazingly, three months later their grades were most closely correlated with the perceived expectation of friends. In other words, students performed at a level consistent with what their friends expected them to perform. Certainly that is less likely to occur in adults, but there is no question that we often permit the values of others to determine our behaviors.

We will not get very motivated by living for the values of other people. Life requires a lot of energy. We are wise not to dissipate our power by failing to be true to our own values. Walking through the fires is just not worth the effort if we are not being true to ourselves. Children who are living out the fantasies of their parents, wives who are living out the dreams of their husbands, husbands who are living according to the desires of their wives are all going to come up short on energy when the going gets tough. When the going gets tough, the only dream worth living for is yours!

It is vitally important to wear your own hat. You are in a position to know what is important to you. Most of us experience some disappointment in midlife because we are not where we thought we would be. We don't have the job security or the savings we thought we would. We can make it anyway, if we have an awareness of what is important to us and have the courage to live according to that. What is inside us truly counts.

Know Your Values

Once we know what our real values are, we can be committed to them. We can move in the directions we want to go. We simply cannot be led by values until we know what they are.

We would expect adults to know what their values are, but it is surprising how few people can clearly articulate their own values. I have often asked groups to take the time to list the five to ten things they value most in life. Never do we go through that exercise without having people scratch their heads and say, "I'm not sure I know."

If you already know your values, you are ahead of a lot of people. If you do not know them, you may be able to discover what is important to you by doing some of the following exercises. Try these exercises whether you know your values or not. The process will either confirm or uncover your real values.

Ask and Act

We don't get answers because we don't ask questions. We don't get helpful answers because we do not ask helpful questions. Ask helpful questions. Ask yourself, "What do I really want to do with my life? What do I want to achieve with my life?" I follow the suggestions of Stephen Covey when I do this exercise.

First, I ask with intent. I want to know so that I can do. I will use the information I get from within to direct my behavior. I ask of myself, "What do I want to do right now? What is right for me right now?" If I listen carefully, I almost always get an answer. I may ask the questions in the form of a prayer, "God, what do you want me to do right now? What is right for me right now?"

The answers usually evolve around my values. I want to live a healthy life. One answer I often get is to either begin or continue an exercise program and/or a good nutritional program. It is right for me to do healthy things.

I want to grow in my knowledge of information, spiritual issues, God, and meaning. So some of my answers revolve around methods for gaining knowledge. This includes reading; writing my thoughts; attending classes; discussing things that are important to me; and perhaps attending a class, school, or seminar. It may include listening to tapes or viewing videos.

I certainly want to establish friendships and good relationships within my family. Answers related to this value will involve activities such as listening to others, spending time with them, and encouraging them consistently.

I want my life to count after I'm gone. I want to leave a legacy. Answers related to this value include helping others, writing my thoughts, encouraging others to be what they believe is best for them. I am writing because I value sharing my thoughts with the hope that this will impact someone in a positive way.

Covey suggests that we ask without excuse. When answers come in the form of things to do, commit to doing them. Avoid saying things such as "I'm too old," "I'm too young," "People won't understand; they may laugh at me." If there is something I want to do related to my own values, I will be wise to approach them without excuse.

Finally, act with courage. Do what you believe is right for you now. Do what you believe God wants you to do and do it now. I wish I had always done that. I wish I would always do it now. I am just thankful to God for this day and the chance to do what I believe is important right now. For now there is hope!

Use Your Imagination

I am again indebted to Covey for reminding me of this exercise. In one form or another, we have used this in groups for many years. The idea is to write your obituary or eulogy. Write what you would like for each of the following to say about you when you are deceased: your family, your friends, your coworkers, your clergyperson. The things you write will more than likely reflect what you think is important. At least they will indicate how you would like to be remembered. Pull from what you write statements that will incorporate the values expressed. Are these things important to you? If they are, you can begin moving toward them right now.

Discover What Is Important

Try writing a list of five things you think are important. Are these the things you are doing? Is this what you are getting out of life? You can answer these questions by putting your list to some tests.

Beside each of the five things, write a note about the last time you did that thing. If you listed a person, when did you last spend time with that person? How often do you spend time with the person or do the thing that you say is important?

Make a second note. Did you value this thing five years ago in the same way as you do now? Do you think you will value this five years in the future? Do you have plans that assure you of getting the thing, achieving the thing, or being in the place or relationship that you say you value? If not, then take the time to make some plans right now.

(1) *Ask yourself some questions:* What do I want to experience more frequently in the future than I have in the past? Do I want to spend less time with some activities that do not contribute to my value? An example might be spending less time watching television or more time reading or relaxing.

(2) *Write a mission statement.* Be as elaborate or as simple as you desire in this kind of exercise. I have simply stated that my mission is to seek first God's will. I believe this leads me to my specified mission: easing the pain of others. Underneath it all, as much as it is possible for me, I want to live with joy.

(3) *Remain true to your magnets.* My mission, my goals, my dreams become the magnets that pull my life toward them. I want to remain true to these magnets. If I do outwardly what I believe inwardly, there is tremendous power in my life. I will be able to walk through the fires of life with determination and not lose my sense of direction. If I have no sense of direction, difficulties will become insurmountable. I will not be motivated to walk on through them. When I know where I want to go, I will be far more highly motivated to go there, in spite of the obstacles.

(4) *Adopt a belief.* Begin to say it to yourself. "I am a person of integrity. I live according to my own values." Talk about it to others. Put it on tape. Write it on cards and place them where you can read them often. "I am a person of integrity. I live according to my own values."

Putting It into Perspective

Years ago I heard a man tell a story of value. He said his family was important to him, and because they were so important, he wanted to earn a good living for them. He did. He became so successful that he moved his office into a city a few hours from his home. He bought an airplane and flew to work on Monday mornings. He returned home on Friday evenings. This successful man began to bring work home on the weekends.

One Saturday morning W. was sitting in his home study. One of his three daughters came in and sat on the floor, drawing a picture on a sheet of paper. "What are you doing, Sweetheart?" "Drawing a butterfly." "That's nice." He went back to work.

W. returned to his office on Sunday. On Tuesday he received a call from his wife. The daughter who had been drawing the picture had become critically ill. She died before he could get home.

A few weeks later, still grieving the loss of the daughter, W. went to his study. He found on his desk a drawing of a butterfly with this note, "Daddy, I love you." That was decision time for W. He determined from that day forward to spend a great deal more time with his family. He began telling them how much they meant to him. W. concluded his comments with something like this, "I can't bring her back, but I can let this tragedy bring me closer to those who remain."

What or who is important to you? Be true to your own values.

CHAPTER 11

Gratitude

I AM FREQUENTLY SURPRISED TO DISCOVER HOW FEW PEOPLE EXPRESS gratitude. Teachers report that, though they help thousands of children through classes at school, seldom do any come back to say, "Thank you." It is as if each one believes the teacher, minister, leader, helper, or friend "owed" him/her everything received. Living without gratitude eventually leads to frustration and dissatisfaction.

Expressing thanks is nice for the person who has done something for us, but the real value comes to the one expressing gratitude. It makes me feel better about myself, and when I feel better about myself, I am more empowered to make it through the fires.

Gladder Than Madder

Gerald Mann tells the story of his parents' rise to affluence and their eventual fall from that pinnacle. It is a wonderful story about the attitude of gratitude.

His parents made enough money to buy a large piece of land in Texas. They built a game preserve where hunters could come for recreation. It was a great idea. The only problem was, a drought occurred the first year, the second, and even the third. Still they would have been alright if they had just gotten some rain.

It rained. It rained and rained and rained. They were flooded out. The family lost most everything they had. What remained was placed in a boat. While his mother and father were towing the boat out to dry land, sightseers in a speed boat zipped by them and tipped the little boat over. Everything was lost.

Gerald said his mother began crying. His father started singing. The louder he sang, the more she cried. Finally, Mr. Mann took his wife by the shoulders and said to her, "Woman, I remember when we didn't have any stuff. Then I remember when we had a lot of stuff. Now we have lost this stuff. I am sure we will get more stuff in the future. But for right now, I am gladder we had it than I am madder that we lost it." What a great attitude of gratitude! Gladder we had it than madder we lost it.

That attitude applies to many things in life. Most of us have been blessed with a lot of material things. Some of us have lost them. Many of us have had some great relationships. Some of us have lost them. Are we gladder or madder?

Glad I Had the Job

A few years ago I had an opportunity to work with two Major League baseball teams. I worked with the St. Louis Cardinals during the 1981 and 1982 seasons. As a result of some misunderstandings, I felt it was wise for me to quit the job during the 1982 World Series. I worked with the team throughout the season, but missed the big finale. That was a real disappointment to me. In some ways, I thought I had been treated unfairly.

I was upset for awhile, and then it finally dawned on me. I had always been a fan of the Cardinals. Now I had had the chance to work with them, be in spring training, be in the clubhouse at every home game, watch the games from the press box, and spend time with a lot of people I admired. In retrospect, I can honestly say I am gladder I had the job than madder that I had to quit the job.

It probably would help any of us who lose a job to recoup energy for continuing to live if we would learn to focus on gratitude for what we have had rather than on the loss.

Glad in Spite of Pain and Loss

I believe the worst fires are those involving diagnosis of serious disease or the loss of someone we love through death. There is no question that these fires bring the heat of grief into our hearts. Nothing will stop some of the pain. We sometimes cannot expect to not hurt. The best we can do is make it through, to persevere.

I learned that lesson again when my father died. It hurt terribly to lose him, but the pain has been lessened by the gratitude I have for thousands of memories. I will continue to celebrate his life with those memories for as long as I live. The same is true of my friend, Dewitt Marzette.

Dewitt was an absolutely magnificent friend. He was a trusted and loyal person, one of the finest Christian men I have ever known. I loved him. He died. When I reflected over the years of friendship, I could honestly say I was much gladder that I had him as a friend than that I lost him. Other friends and his family share the same sentiment. Our attitude of gratitude enabled us to make it through the loss without being devastated. We grieved, but not as those with no hope. We grieved him and celebrated him at the same time.

I have counseled about a thousand cancer patients over the past fifteen years. They are hurting people. They are feeling the pressure. Some of them are so courageous that they help me. Others begin the time we spend together with despair. I try to delicately point them in the direction of hope and gratitude. They certainly feel better when the focus of their lives is changed to plans for the future and gratitude for the past. They are empowered to make it through the present with a shift in focus.

Glad in Spite of Failure

Who of us has not had failures? To focus on them is to weaken our resolve for the future. When we experience failure, it is a good time to remember better times with gratitude. I am thankful for my successes. Thankfulness helps me walk through my failures with hope.

My marriage of thirty-eight years ended in divorce. It was a painful time for me. I never expected it. Oh, there were problems. We both contributed to them, but I just believed we would go on together anyway. It was not to be.

At first I focused on the loss of a dream, the loss of an illusion. I am sure I was grieving more for what I hoped would be than for what was. The point is, I was hurting and grieving. The grieving did not change until I started looking at what I had.

From my marriage I have four wonderful children—two fine young men and two fine young women. They have brought into my life five grandchildren, so far! They have brought more joy to me than

I could have ever imagined possible as I grew up. I have been blessed. I am gladder for what I have than madder for what I have lost.

During my marriage I was able to get a good education. I started with a high school diploma and a '47 Chevy. I have now a B.A., two masters degrees, and a Ph.D. from a school I dreamed of attending from the days of high school. I have lived in nice places and driven nice cars. (I have driven a few clunkers, too.) I can honestly say I am gladder I have had things than madder that I don't. When we focus on gratitude, we are empowered to walk through the fires.

Become Gladder

There are some things over which we have very little control. The ability to give thanks or express gratitude is not one of them. This is certainly something we control. Begin to see yourself as someone who expresses thanks. Write notes to people, make telephone calls, say thank you when you have a chance.

Jesus Christ healed ten men of leprosy, a disease that forced people to be isolated from society, alone and rotting away. Surely that was such a great thing that all of the ten would be overwhelmed with gratitude. No! Only one returned to say thank you. The percentage hasn't changed much, if at all. One in ten! But to that one comes the power to be a real fire walker.

Say it over and over to yourself: I am a person who is grateful. Remind yourself and others. Let's be grateful. Let's be gladder that we have had and will have good than madder that we have lost anything. Be thankful, and peace will possess your heart.

CHAPTER 12
Humor

My sense of humor is my "seventh sense." It is one of my most important coping tools. In fact, it is a permanent part of my personal mission statement, which is summed up like this: "I will seek the kingdom of God and His will first in my life. I will seek to alleviate human suffering whereever I find it. I will have as much fun as I can."

Jesus Christ came to give life, and to give it full of joy (John 15:11). If we believe this, how can we not seek as much joy and fun as possible? The secular minds know it. Neitzhe said that man, the most suffering animal, created laughter. The humorist knows it. Josh Billings said, "There isn't much fun in medicine, but there is a whole lot of medicine in fun."

Everything works better when it is greased with humor. People who have fun have a greater passion for life and are more energetic, healthier, and even more productive.

The ability to laugh at ourselves and our situations is so powerful as a coping tool that it should be a required course included in education and training. Think of all the things that are made easier and more tolerable by humor.

A Great Stress Reliever

When my family moved into a church parsonage in 1959, we inherited a leaky roof. In fact, "leaky" is an understatement. When the rain fell outside, we had to put pans all over the bedroom. The plinking sounds of dripping water played musical tunes that were irritants to our ears.

One night, during a freezing snow and ice storm, the drainpipe froze solid. Water from the collecting snow backed up under the roof and melted. This resulted in a midnight bedroom shower. I thought of the Ancient Mariner, "Water, water everywhere and the bed did sink."

I made the brilliant observation that the drainpipe had to come down. My wife agreed. We put on robes, pulled out a ladder and the only tool I really needed at that moment—a chopping ax! I orchestrated the propping of the ladder in a strategic position so that I could climb up, lean out over the porch railing, and, literally, chop the drainpipe down.

In the middle of this process, I looked down at my wife. Her robe was blowing in the snowy wind. She was openly crying. I said, "Hey, we'll be laughing about this in a couple of years." She was undaunted, "Well, it sure isn't funny now."

She was right. So was I! We have told and embellished that story many times to the delight of our family and friends. The fact is, the note of humor helped us through a stressful moment. If we develop the ability to project ourselves into the future, we can laugh at a present crisis. Humor helps us deal with stress. I have listed for myself several "stress-busting humor ideas." Try some of them the next time you are feeling stressed. Add to the list for yourself.

- Look through a fork, and pretend that people are in jail.
- Write a note about your feelings, but write it in pig-Latin. Atwha oda ouya inktha?
- Write a story using alphabet soup.
- Fill out a check using Roman numerals.
- Wear a sloppy sweatshirt to the mall, and watch the stressed people walk by.

Help in Accepting Our Own Frailties

We are all so fallible that we had better learn to laugh at ourselves. If we take ourselves too seriously, we will be in constant battles defending our errors and trying to justify ourselves. Why not just develop the ability to laugh and go on? I find it essential.

I often speak without using notes. As a result, I do a lot of ad-libbing. One Sunday I decided on the spur of the moment to jibe the congregation by saying that some of them were trying to float into heaven on their Beautyrest mattresses. I thought it would be a "cute" way of telling them that they needed to do a little more work. It didn't come out the way I had planned. Perhaps I just got my television commercials mixed up. I said, "Some of you are trying to get to heaven by floating in your Maidenforms." After a pause, there was nervous laughter, then a roar. Later, one woman took delight in telling me that she dreamed she "came to church in her Maidenform."

That was thirty years ago, and I still have an occasional reminder. There was no defense. I goofed. I might as well laugh. The fires of failure are hot enough. We can cool them a little by laughing at ourselves.

Help in Alleviating Pain

Norman Cousins, in *Anatomy of an Illness,* said that during his illness, he discovered that ten minutes of laughter would give him two hours of pain-free rest. The reason? Laughter releases natural painkillers (endorphins) into our systems. Humor helps our bodies respond more positively to disease. In *You Can Fight for Your Life,* LeShan says our immune systems respond best when we are in touch with the joy of living.

My friend, Hugh, graduated from high school apparently headed for a fine career. He attended an Ivy League school. He later became a pilot in the Strategic Air Command. He then resigned his commission and entered law school.

One night, after studying late with a friend, he fell asleep while driving back to his room. His Volkswagen went off a mountain road. It was hours before he was found. His spinal cord was severed. He was paralyzed for the rest of his life.

I called him during a visit to our hometown. After someone handed him the telephone, I spoke, "Hello, Hugh. This is Bill." He responded with his characteristic hesitation, "Why . . . er . . . Bill. It's good to hear from you." Then I asked what seemed to me a dumb question. "How are you doing?"

He seemed to enjoy the question. It gave him a chance to respond with tongue in check. "Not too well. You see . . . er . . . I had a little accident a little over twenty years ago, and I haven't quite recovered from it yet. Looks like I . . . er . . . will miss another track season."

We both laughed. His sense of humor helped him to survive for more than thirty years. He inspired me and helped me to see again the value of humor in walking through the fires of adversity.

One patient, suffering from an inner ear infection, was literally holding on to the side of his bed because the room seemed to be spinning. When asked how he was doing, he responded, "Not too badly, really. This is probably the cheapest way to get drunk." He was not even a drinker, but he chose to frame his misery in humor.

When we are ill, we would be wise to remember Voltaire's statement, "The art of medicine consists of amusing the patient while nature cures the disease." Laugh. You reduce the power of illness when you do.

Help in Dealing with Aging

One friend said that the older he became, the less importance he placed on importance. In other words, life is too important to be taken seriously. A lady said, "I knew I was getting old one day when I stooped over to tie my shoe laces and actually said to myself, 'I wonder if there is anything else I can do while I'm down here?' " People who frame aging in a funny frame can honestly follow Browning in growing old because they know with him that "the best is yet to be."

Help in Dealing with Divorce

While involved in a divorce, one woman said, "I'll never be able to find anyone else. I am a failure. This is awful." She felt miserable and had a hard time dealing with the whole process. Another, in a similar situation said, "Well, now that this is really over, maybe I can find someone who actually deserves me." She didn't feel quite so miserable. I know this is not a total solution. The fires of divorce burn scorchingly hot for anyone, but it helps if we permit ourselves to find some humor to lessen the pain.

Help in Any Area of Life

In the movie *Mr. Holland's Opus*, Mr. Holland tells a young clarinet player that he can teach her to read notes from the paper, but she will never learn to play music until it becomes fun to her.

When I worked with the St. Louis Cardinals in the 1982 baseball season, I remember talking to a discouraged Darrell Porter. It was mid to late August, and Darrell was struggling with the game. We had a long talk about the problems he was having. I reminded him that, even though baseball was a job for him, it was still a game and was to be enjoyed.

He had starting arriving late at the park and trying to get out early. I suggested he come early and plan to stay late. I also suggested he get out on the field and have fun before the game. I watched from the press box as Darrell had fun before the game. He went to the mound and pitched to a teammate for a few minutes. He enjoyed the game. He played better and turned his season around, partly because he was having fun again. Incidently, Darrell won the most valuable player honors in both the playoffs and the World Series that year. Having fun can make you perform better too.

Humor in Religion

No, it is not sacrilegious to think of God as having a sense of humor. You might not think this is true when you look into the sour faces of some of the "faithful." The fact is, religious leaders from every denominational background have given us wonderful humorous quips about life. Even Confucius is credited with humor, though he would have had to live a hundred years and talk twenty-four hours a day to have said everything he is credited with saying.

Jesus was no piker at quips either. Consider the humor implied when he was confronted with the haughty and pompous Pharisees. They came to him with judgmental attitudes. He must have had a twinkle in his eyes when he asked, "How can you see to remove a speck from another's eye when you have a beam sticking out of yours?" Then there was the day when Jesus was surrounded by the egotistical religious leaders (like our preachers, priests, or rabbis). I can imagine he was nearly giggling when he said, "The prostitutes will get into heaven before you people do." On second thought, that might not be so funny.

There is humor in church too. We asked for a secret ballot naming five people from our church to be nominated as deacons. We suggested that people look for the names of people who were filled with the Holy Spirit. One ballot came back with no names on it. It simply had the comment, "I don't know the good people of this church well enough to know what they are full of." There is humor in religion.

Fire Walking

The wonderful Baptist humorist, Grady Nutt, tried to help us deal with racial prejudice and theological conflict with humor. He labeled prejudice as ignorant. He used a blatant example to prove his point. "Jewish prejudice against the Gentiles was so great that if a fish was caught off the shore of Gentile territory, it was considered unclean. If the fish had the energy to swim a few feet further and the same fish was caught downstream, it was considered clean and could be eaten." He suggested that our racial prejudice was about as sensible as that.

Another Lesson from My Dad

My dad was in the hospital for surgery. Neither we nor he knew how serious it might be. One day as I began a visit with him, I asked the standard, "How are you doing?" He was in pain but rolled his eyes and looked at me saying, "Why, Bill, I guess I must be sick. I can't think of any other reason why they'd have me here in this hospital." We both laughed, and he seemed to feel better. Feeling better, he went on, "And say, if I'm ever sick again, don't bring me here. Do you know that 'prackly' (his word for practically) everyone here is sick. There is no telling what I might catch."

When he had a stroke a few years later, he was being examined in the emergency room of a local hospital. The doctor, examining the muscles in his face, said, "Can you smile, Mr. Little?" Dad answered, "If I could think of something funny, I could."

My dad said he measured his success by the amount of fun he had. One day he said to me, "I've had quite a bit of fun. There is not much about my life I would change." He never lost his sense of humor. It helped him walk through the fires of illness and pain.

If we develop a real belief in humor, we can learn to have fun. Experiences are filtered through our beliefs. When we believe life is hard and serious, we will have very little fun. When we believe that life is meant to be fun, we will filter our experiences through that belief and find a lot more fun than most people find. If we learn to laugh at ourselves, we will always have live entertainment nearby. Look for humor. Believe you can learn to have fun. I am going to have as much fun in my life as I can. It helps me to walk through the fires.

CHAPTER 13
Celebration

WHEN WE WALK THROUGH THE FIRES, WE WILL FEEL A LOT LESS HEAT if we learn to celebrate every experience. I am not being naive when I say "every" experience. Certainly we all have to admit there are some very painful experiences in life, and I am not suggesting that we deny the pain. I am simply suggesting that the way through the pain is a lot easier if we learn to celebrate.

Without becoming unrealistic, we can see there are ways to find the positive in all of life's experiences. Failure is an example. I do not celebrate the fact that I fail. I do not like failure at all, but I have learned there are reasons to rejoice in what I learn from my failures. If I fail to learn when I fail, I have failed indeed.

Again, without meaning to be glib about it, I do believe that every time I make an error in life, I have found another way not to do what I am trying to do. That leads to my belief that the best definition of insanity is: continuing to do the same things in the same way and expecting different results—which is the failure to learn.

Celebrate Despite Failed Marriage

Look at the number of people who have experienced some kind of failure in their marriages. Most of them get back into another marriage and make the same mistakes again. Often there are second, third, and even fourth marriages. Some are just unhappy and decide to live out their lives in silent misery.

Few of these people have celebrated their failed relationships. They have felt the pain. They have lived with reduced productivity. They have been depressed. They have been angry. But few have added the concept of celebration.

I am sorry my first marriage ended in divorce. I would be sorrier still if I wound up in an equally unhappy mismatch. I celebrate the things I learned. I do not want to make those mistakes again.

Celebrate Despite Death

Some of the most agonizing moments in life are the moments when we walk through the fires of death. I would not for one moment discount that pain nor desecrate the memory of one precious life. I would, however, point out that we often do a great disservice to our departed friends and loved ones by not celebrating their lives even while we grieve their deaths.

My father was one of my dearest friends. I hardly ever give a lecture that I do not share some of what I learned from him. I had the unique opportunity of delivering the message at his funeral. I remembered with the people at his funeral service the things he had said about being successful and learned again the value of relationships and the relative insignificance of things. Of course it was a time of grieving, but it was much more. It was also a time of rejoicing.

I rejoiced with my family and friends that my dad (I called him "Daddy" or his initials, "E. T.") was no longer suffering from the stroke that had left him helpless and speechless for the last six months of his life. I rejoiced at the memories we shared. He was one of the most fun people I have ever known.

His last intelligible words were humorous. Out of one side of his mouth he mumbled, "Bill, get me that walker in from the bedroom." I knew he was momentarily disoriented. "You're not at home, E. T." He tried to raise an eyebrow. It was his sign of recognition that he had made a mistake, and it was the closest thing to an admission of error that we usually got from him. He said, "No, I'm not home. But I would be if you'd get me that walker." He tried to smile. I could see it in his eyes. I don't remember understanding another message from him. I just cherish his remarkable sense of humor. I celebrated his life.

Celebrate and Rejoice

Jesus taught that we should rejoice even when we are persecuted for doing right. Paul said to "rejoice in all things." Jesus said he came that we might have abundant life. What gives us the ability to celebrate and rejoice?

(1) *Believe in yourself.* The knowledge that we can do a certain thing gives us the courage to attempt it. The examples are plentiful and familiar to most of us. One of the most common examples is that of running the four-minute mile. Men tried and tried to break under four minutes in the mile run. They could not. Many believed it was humanly impossible to achieve this goal. There was, however, at least one man, Jim Ryan, who believed it could be done. He trained and trained, and then he did it. No one had ever achieved that feat before, but once it was done, it was repeated time after time. When the deep belief was that it could not be done, no one did it. It was not a matter of ability but of belief.

We have the capacity to rejoice and celebrate life after tragedies. I have seen people do it, and I have done it myself. When my wife divorced me, I was devastated. My energy was low, but I was able to keep on walking. I did my jobs. Then I learned that life could be full again. It could be fuller than it had been before. I began to celebrate life. I honestly believe my life is better today than it has ever been. I thank God for the ability to celebrate.

When my father died, I felt the pain of loss keenly. He was one of my best friends. I talked to him often and traveled repeatedly with him. Still I was able to continue celebrating his life. I refused to permit my pain to blur the joy of all he had been and would continue to be for me. I did not wallow in self-pity, but by the grace of God was able to celebrate his life even in my grief. I deeply believed I could, and I did.

You can again find the strength and grace to celebrate and rejoice, no matter what has happened to you. I ask you to believe it is possible, because only then will you give yourself the freedom to celebrate and rejoice in life again.

(2) *Maintain a sense of humor.* Never forget how to smile and laugh. It has been said that a smile is the light in the window of your face that lets people know you are at home. It is also the way to release great powers of healing and survival.

Humor certainly can be a source of healing when we are grieving. Barbara Johnson has illustrated this concept in her books. It is hard to imagine the pain she has experienced in seeing one son nearly killed in an accident, losing one son in Vietnam, and losing another son in a collision with a drunken driver. Her books reflect the ability to find enough humor in life to keep going.

She quoted some confused medical conclusions from Dr. Gott in her book, *"Mama, Get the Hammer! There's a Fly on Papa's Head"* She said some patients described their doctors as saying they had, " 'migrating' headaches, 'prospect' gland problems, 'mental' pause, or they needed a 'scat' scan of the brain. One man mentioned that some-one quit breathing and had to have artificial 'insemination.' A woman had to have a 'monotone' of her breast, and another complained of pain in the 'palms' of her feet."

Collecting such humor and sharing it is one way to continue the process of rejoicing and celebrating life, even after the bad times. "Humor is like changing a baby's diapers. It does not permanently solve the problem, but it makes the present situation more tolerable."

(3) *Remember to sing.* Music is the language of the soul. It is a con-stant in a roller coaster world. One of the things I like about going to church is that the people there are always singing. There I sing when I'm happy, when I'm sad, and when I'm just there. I can sing no mat-ter what my outward circumstances. I can sing because I believe I can. My singing probably wouldn't help everyone. Some might even find it depressing. So I sing in groups, in the car, in the shower, and outside when I'm alone. My singing is for me and me alone. I am not doing it for a performance.

Many people have forgotten to sing and listen to music. There is no music in a lot of lives, which is sad. We can sing through the fires of life if we really believe we can. It is one way to celebrate during times of affliction.

(4) *Learn to find the poetry.* Some of us like to write poetry. We don't often share it because, like our art work, we don't think it is good enough to show to others. I love writing poetry, but even more I love to sense the poetry in life. When I am hurting, I can find poetry in life to ease my pain. In the afternoon shadows, I wrote these words:

It was bright and clean when the morning sun rose—
The day was fresh as every child of beginning knows.
Dew sparkled on the flowers, and there were blue skies
When today awoke and rubbed the sleep from her eyes.
Plans were made, and promises were to be kept,
But soon disappointed people, empty-handed wept.
We must do what we can in the sun's bright heat,
For in the shadows of evening, intention sounds retreat.
Then today will yawn and go again to its bed;
Tomorrow sets the alarm, but this day is dead!

I sat on the front porch of a cousin's home in eastern Mississippi and listened to the night. I was thinking of relatives I loved who were not at the family reunion that night. I celebrated as I wrote:

The sounds of night in orange moonlight,
Crickets from the thickets in strange harmony—
It's still and quiet, and it seems to be right
As the stillness penetrates to the soul of me.
The sounds of the city in a staccato ditty, clash—
The noise of cars and the sounds of industry,
The speed and the noise penetrate to the soul of me.
Perhaps there's a way to enhance the chance for peace,
If I can hold in my soul what God can release.
Then in the noise and the ever-quickening paces,
My life can become a quiet green oasis.

These writings and the three to four thousand others I have written may not say much to anyone else, but they are the celebration of moments in my life—moments where the poetry was louder than the pain and pressure. I hear it because I deeply believe I can hear it. Can you hear it? If you believe you can, you can.

(5) *Remain conscious.* I like to be conscious, I mean really conscious. I like to smell, touch, hear, and see the world in which I live. I agree with my father's thoughts about being awake. He said he would never sleep if he didn't just have to for health's sake. He said, "You miss everything that's going on when you are asleep, and life is so

short that I hate to miss anything." Life is too short to be unconscious through one hour of it.

We can deal with pain by becoming conscious of the process of pain. The next time you have to deal with pain and cannot or do not want to get pain medication, try becoming conscious of the way your body is reacting to pain. Follow the pain from the point of hurt into the nerves and into the brain and back to the point of hurting. This process often eases the pain.

An option is to become conscious of other things at the time of your hurting. Focus on the world outside your pressure. Think of things you can do or things that are happening around you. This conscious diversion is one way to walk through fires.

(6) *Find peace even in the storm.*

The Eye of the Storm

I stood in the quiet in the eye of the storm
Where in calm a hazy truth took form.
Even when winds of confusion round me blow,
There is a peace that my soul can know.
For at the heart of every battle, every strife,
There is that key to security for life.
Somehow assurance lives in the storm's silent eye,
And a deep serenity of courage refuses to die.
It lives in a quietness reserved for the tomb.
It lives like a baby curled in the womb.
It is the anchor of determination that glows,
Even surrounded by the fiercest wind that blows.
It says, "No matter what comes I can take it.
No matter how hard the way I can make it."
For in hurricanes such hope is still not dead,
Where a tree bowed by the wind raises its head.
With knowledge that life goes on safe from harm,
This is peace that comes in the eye of the storm.

Celebration

Celebrate!

I celebrate because I am alive.
I celebrate because I believe in God.
I celebrate because I love life.
I celebrate in good times and bad.
I celebrate because it is in my soul to celebrate.

Repeat it to yourself. Paraphrase it anyway that is meaningful to you. Imagine yourself celebrating in all kinds of circumstances. Once we have accepted the fact that there is pain in life, we can celebrate.

CHAPTER 14
Internal Control

IF WE LEARN TO CONTROL A PERSON'S THOUGHTS, WE CONTROL THAT person. If we learn to control our own thoughts, we control ourselves. Thoughts are expressed in terms of "self-talk." In the book of James we are taught that if we control the tongue, we control the whole body. I take those words to mean that if we control what we say, either to ourselves or to others, we control our lives. We influence ourselves most in the internal dialogue.

Controlling Our Thoughts and Emotions

The practitioners of rational emotive or cognitive therapy have taught us for years that it is not what happens to us that determines our attitudes and actions, but rather what we say to ourselves about what happens to us.

I often say I have never lost a moment's sleep over what others have said about or to me, but I have lost hours and hours of sleep over what I have said to myself about what others have said concerning me or to me. I say to myself things such as, "I wish I had said . . ." " I wonder what was meant by that." "Next time I will say . . ." I change my consequence by changing what I say to myself. That is one form of internal control.

I am able to walk through the fires of criticism, name calling, misunderstanding, and so on when I learn to control my internal thoughts or self-talk.

Paul wrote in Phillipians 4 that we are to think on positive things. Earlier he said we are to have the mind in us that was in Christ. We are to think as he thought. Such suggestions are meaningless unless we can control our thoughts.

Thoughts are the parents of our emotions. We can certainly influence, if not totally control, our emotions by controlling our thoughts. We will be much more effective in walking through the fire of grief, depression, or frustration when we exercise internal control or influence of our emotions.

Anger is also controlled internally. Anger is usually a secondary emotion. In other words, we usually feel something else first, then we feel anger. An example would be when someone cuts us off in traffic and we come close to having an accident. We generally express anger at "that fool" who is going to kill someone. What we probably feel first is fear. We seldom say, "Wow, that really frightened me"—which would be dealing with the primary emotion. We usually deal with the secondary emotion, anger. Perhaps we find it more acceptable to be angry than afraid.

We often "lose" our tempers. Or do we? I have lost my temper at home only to have the phone ring. In the midst of my "lost" temper, I pick up the phone and with complete control say, "Hello." I have more control than I usually recognize or want to admit. I believe we "use" our tempers more than we "lose" them. We have internal control if we choose to use it.

Circles of Control

Dealing with areas of control is one of the most helpful concepts I have ever discovered. In my book, *This Will Drive You Sane,* I called this "problem location." In order to deal with a problem effectively, I have to first discover whose problem it is. I have wasted a lot of time internalizing other people's problems.

The most common way of expressing this concept is through what is called the "serenity prayer." It is the prayer that God will help us to have the courage to change the things we can change, accept the things we cannot change, and have the wisdom to know the difference. The modern-day application of this principle is Stephen Covey's "circles of control," which I discussed in chapter 3.

Consider this example. Whether or not I lose my job is frequently outside my area of control. I can put in my time and do my best to do a good job, but I cannot control the numbers. My circle of control is how I work on a daily basis and what I will do if I am cut from the work force. When I focus on loss, I am weakened. My energy flows inward. I feel tired. When I focus on what I can do, I am strengthened. I feel energized. I want to live more and more of my life in my own circle.

Another example comes from a recent visit I had with my daughter, Caron. We were having a cup of coffee one morning when Jane, a neighbor of hers, came screaming up the street. She sounded absolutely desperate, as if someone had just been killed.

Caron went out to see what the problem was and returned in a few minutes to tell me that her friend's husband had just come in the house on his lunch break and announced he was leaving. The wife was shocked and devastated. She became hysterical. My daughter asked if I would mind going to the neighbor's home to see if I could help her. I didn't mind, so I was soon sitting in the backyard of an emotionally distraught woman.

After listening to her cry and vent her fears and feelings for about ten minutes, I asked Jane, "What can you do about the situation?" She did not know of anything she could do. I asked for a piece of paper and drew a circle design. I wrote the words "control" and "no control" in the appropriate places and asked her to tell me which circle her situation was in. She quickly responded that it was in the circle of "no control."

I asked Jane the second question, "Then what *can* you do?" She responded, "I don't know of anything." I suggested, "You can make plans for what you will do when he comes back." Her expression changed, "Do you think he will come back?" "They usually do." That doesn't mean that people come back to stay or that the problems will be solved, but when someone just leaves on the spur of the moment, they usually have second thoughts. He did.

We talked for a few minutes about what she could do if or when he came back. Then we started talking about other things she could do that day. Some of those things were not related to the present problem at all. I have discovered that people feel better when they think of things they can do rather than remaining obsessed over things that are beyond their control.

In a few minutes this young woman told me I could go home. She said she knew what she could do. I wondered what she might mean. I think I felt a little uneasy with her shift in mood. She told me she knew things to do. She said, "Well, for one thing, I can wash my face. I can comb my hair. I can put on some make-up. And I can walk across the street and have some coffee with you and Caron." She could and she did! That certainly did not solve her problems, but it did restore her to a place where she felt a little energy and was able to step out of the hysteria.

Decision making is an internal process we control. We certainly can learn to ask ourselves good questions. When faced with decisions about our behavior, we would be wise to ask, "What results do I want?" Let the answer to this question guide decisions. We are wise to ask, "Which circle is this in?" We are helped to deal with life's pressures when we identify the things we can and cannot do. Victims are never as energized as participants.

An Issue for Cancer Patients

When someone is given a diagnosis of cancer, they feel a loss of control. This feeling has been verbalized to me this way: "I feel like I am dying, and there is nothing I can do. I just have to turn myself over to medical people and let them do whatever they can for me and to my body. I am even afraid of the treatment."

Certainly there are some justifiable feelings there. I try never to minimize the situation because it is a terrible one, but people are empowered by some restoration of control, even if it is in some small area. One of the first things I do with patients is try to help them regain some perception of control by moving them into things they can do. This is usually done by pointing out to the patients that, while we cannot change the diagnosis, we can begin to do some things that will help them live better and have a better chance to respond positively to treatment.

I recommend activities such as gathering information to help in the decision-making process, listening to relaxation tapes to help them rest better, improving nutrition habits, beginning a moderate exercise program, planning for some fun things to do with family or friends, focusing on goals for the future, and getting in touch with their spiritual foundations. These are things they "can do." By moving into the area of internal control, patients are better able to walk through the fires of fear and grief.

Practice Internal Control

Learn to say to yourself, "I have internal control. I make decisions about my behaviors, my emotions, and my attitudes." This is closely related to being a responsible person. I am responsible for my decisions, and I do have internal control. Write the belief. Talk about it to others. Practice it.

For years we have heard people in the workplace respond to a request for work, "I don't do that. It is not in my area." We can apply and practice internal control in a positive way. "I will do that or this because it *is* in my circle of control. I will not worry about that or this because it *is not* in my circle of control. Internal control is a powerful tool enabling me to walk through the fires of life.

CHAPTER 15
Passion

LIFE IS EXCITING. FAILURE TO RECOGNIZE THIS FACT IS SURE TO ROB US of wonderful blessings. Life is more thrilling than a playoff football game. How can we sit on our hands when our favorite team is playing? Life is filled with more enthusiasm than a national sales meeting. Life is filled with more passion than real live Romeos and Juliets.

I can think of at least three great benefits derived from living life enthusiastically. Certainly all three of these results of passionate living will help us in walking through the fires.

High Energy Levels

If you are willing to run one simple experiment, you can discover the power of passion. Let me prepare you for the experiment with this brief background. Years ago I taught at a business college. Every morning I heard the class next door to mine shouting in unison at the top of their voices, "Oh boy, am I enthusiastic!" It was early in the morning, and the loud shout often annoyed me. I finally asked the teacher of the class what they were trying to prove or accomplish. She said, "When people act and speak as if they are enthusiastic, they will be enthusiastic." There is more truth than hype in that statement, though I modify it to conclude, "They are more likely to be enthusiastic."

Now for the experiment. Try this. Slump down in your chair, bow your head, close your eyes, and in a soft monotone say, "Oh boy, am I enthusiastic." Feel energized? Probably not. Next, sit up straight in your chair, hold your head up, open your eyes, and in a loud voice with feeling shout, "Oh boy, am I enthusiastic!" Feel more energy? When we live with passion and enthusiasm, we are more energized.

Another thought may help clarify this concept. Imagine that you are lying in bed at 5:30 A.M. The alarm sounds. You have to go to the income tax office for an audit, after which you are scheduled for a root canal. Then, if time permits, you will go in to work. Ever had a day like that? Were you filled with energy and ready to bounce out of bed? Even thinking about such a day can make us tired.

It's the same time of day. The alarm goes off. You are scheduled to begin a long-awaited vacation today. You have an expense-paid trip to a wonderful resort. It is time to go. Do you feel more energy?

The enthusiasm and passion for something we want to do will generate more energy. It stands to reason then that we are better able to cope with life if we learn to face it with passion.

Walter Russell said that one of the keys to success in life is learning to live with passion. I have learned that the secret is not in doing only the things I love, but loving the things I do. That excites and energizes me.

Better Health

Years ago I was in New York City for a meeting with treatment people from all over the world. We were discussing ways to fight cancer. I was especially excited about the opportunity to sit in on a discussion led by Lawrence LeShan. His book *You Can Fight for Your Life* and Simonton's *Getting Well Again* inspired me to begin working with cancer patients.

LeShan talked about really loving life. He suggested that when we become ill with any disease, we are asking our immune systems to fight for our health. He said it is as if we say to our immune systems, "Help me fight this disease so I can live." The imaginary dialogue was as follows:

Immune system: "Why?"

Us: "We want to live?"

Immune system: "Why?"

Us: "Because we have a lot of people depending on us. We have a lot of duties to fulfill. We are not finished with all our work and responsibility."

Immune system: "Bleeeeee."

The conversation can be quite different according to Dr. LeShan. We may say to our immune systems that we want help in getting well. Then this conversation might follow:

Immune system: "Why?"

Us: "We want to live."

Immune system: "Why?"

Us: "Because we love living. We just love to live."

Immune system, with fist thrust high at the top of our bodies: "O. K. Let's get going."

LeShan was making the point that our whole system works better when we enjoy living. We are more energized when we have passion for living. I put this principle to the test with a cancer patient who was in my office recently.

He was a soft-spoken, gentle sort who spoke in a monotone. I asked him, "What excites you?" He responded in his characteristic soft monotone. I wasn't convinced. We spent several minutes talking about joy and excitement and how they energize our immune systems. I then told him about the man who was waiting to see me next. He had been a spiritless, apathetic person just two months ago, but he had changed. I wanted this patient to meet someone who had been down the same road but had regained excitement about life.

We came out of my office, and I introduced the two men. I was not disappointed. Charles had just come from radiation therapy. He was tired and in some pain, but his spirit was not dampened. I asked, "How are you doing today?" Charlie said, "Oh, I'm a little tired, but I'm paddling my own canoe." He then grinned broadly and blurted out, "Just think. Two months ago I couldn't even spell canoe, and now I'm paddling one." He is excited about life.

What is the result of Charlie's excitement? He is doing better than expected in treatment. He has not lost his ability to eat. He is able to continue regular activities with breaks for rest. He is actually having fun with life and looking forward to finishing radiation so that he can, in his words, "get up a full head of steam." I believe Charlie will be with us for a long time to come.

Greater Personal Success

I do not want to become one of the barkers for high power sales conventions, but I want to be honest enough to admit that sales seminars sell because they work. When people become more enthusiastic about a product, they are much more likely to sell it. When we become enthusiastic about anything we do, we will be able to do it with more proficiency.

Success is measured in different ways. In America, we usually measure success by the accumulation of money, property, and notable achievement. There are other measures of success.

Triumphant living is successful living. Anyone who is able to live life that gives personal satisfaction and peace must be considered successful. Anyone who is able to give creative expression to life in greater quantities than he/she takes away from the creativity of others must be considered successful.

Winning is successful. I am not talking about games but about life. I heard Robert Eliot say that the short form of stress tests is simply the question, "Are you winning in life?" He said most people have a pretty good sense of that question. Most of us know if we are winning in life. I believe we are winning if we are living lives we love.

I watched a television special on people who have had "spontaneous remissions" of cancer. Each person had become committed to living life the way they really wanted to live it. They had become enthusiastic about doing the things that were fulfilling to them.

Success can be the freedom to put our own thumbprints on the world, to live with a conscious awareness that we are unique and valuable people. Enthusiasm results.

Practice Living with Passion

Enthusiasm empowers us to cope with the fires of life. Without becoming a mindless Pollyanna, we can find joy and excitement in the challenges of daily living. It isn't that we are enthused about walking through another fire. Rather, we have another fire to walk through, and we know we are much more likely to make it through if we walk with enthusiasm and joy.

Repeat it many times each day: "I live with passion. I am excited to be alive. I love life." We may want to do as the classs at the business college did and repeat daily, "Oh boy, am I enthusiastic!" Become conscious of the enthusiasm or lack of it in others, and encourage people to be more excited about life.

Passion and enthusiasm are so contagious that we can catch it from ourselves. Certainly it is contagious enough for us to catch it from one another. Be enthusiastic about life. Associate with enthusiastic, passionate people. They will energize you. Even difficult tasks are made possible by enthusiasm and joy. Look at Jesus, "the pioneer and perfecter of our faith, who for the sake of the joy that was set before him endured the cross, disregarding its shame, and has taken his seat at the right hand of the throne of God" (Heb 12:2). The light of God is waiting at the end of the tunnel for those who live with passion the abundant life. Passion gives us energy to walk through the fires of life.

CHAPTER 16
Love

LOVE IS THE ONLY REAL REASON FOR LIVING. LOVE DOES NOT OCCUR by accident. It is a result of decisions and commitments. Love takes time. If you want to express love, you must spend time. Don't substitute the idea of "quality" for "quantity" of time. There is no substitute for time. Love is a four-letter word that is often spelled t-i-m-e. Taking time to be with the people you love not only helps them to cope, it also energizes you for living through the fires. When people permit us to love them, they give to us. This line from a song says it well: "I never feel so given to as when you take from me." The results of giving and receiving love are countless.

Gives Positive Energy

Tom recently told me of a conversation with his daughter, Susan, a woman in her thirties who has three children. Her oldest child is a girl, Mary, who is eleven years old. Mary is in constant trouble and receives frequent punishment. Susan admits she really doesn't like the girl and will be glad when she is gone. Tom shook his head sadly as he related the story. Looking at the floor he concluded, "I said to my daughter, 'For God's sake, Susan, you have tried everything else with that girl. Why in hell don't you just hug her?' " Susan refuses to give her daughter any affection. This scenario is far too typical and a very sad commentary. Children who receive little or no loving affection will be ill-equipped to give it to their children and will grow up discouraged and probably misbehaving.

I can only hope and pray that we all will both give and receive more loving hugs from our family and friends. Try hugging your child, your parent, your spouse, or your friend. Like the waters of the pool of Siloam, there is healing in hugs.

When my youngest son was eighteen years old, he and I went to a movie together. As we walked toward the ticket office, Russ put his arm around me. I responded by giving him a big hug, right there in the parking lot. He smiled at me as if he was embarrassed and said, "I could use about eighteen of those every day."

Love really is a source of positive energy. To feel loved, to be hugged, to be noticed by a caring person gives us strength to cope with some of the greatest pressures of life. The absence of those things brings the loss of energy, sickness, and even death.

Empowers Us

Discouragement is one of the major problems of society. When people feel unloved, they feel discouraged and often lose motivation. Problems are often created by people who feel unloved. Show me a successful person, and I will show you someone who has probably been clearly loved. The need is apparent.

A teacher once told me about a young man who was abused by his parents. He was difficult in class most of the time, but especially on a day after he had experienced physical abuse at home. One day little Calvin was misbehaving at an especially high level. The teacher took him aside and said to him, "Calvin, what am I going to do with you." The little guy (a fifth grader) responded, "Don't do nothing with me. Just love me." The teacher did. Calvin was eventually taken out of the home where he was abused. I do not know what ever happened to him, but I know he expressed a genuine need. Calvin could make it through the fires of abuse if he had someone to love him.

We don't have to be loved by a great many people in order to be empowered in life. Sometimes just one person really loving us is enough to help us through. I was fortunate to have a special relation- ship with a grandmother. She loved me unconditionally. I am sure I have made it through a lot of the challenges in my life simply because I knew I was greatly loved by her. There were others who have loved me, but I was most empowered by her love because it was so uncondi- tional. She loved me no matter what I did. When I "messed up," she believed I "messed up" better than anyone else could have. I don't think she doted over me, but it was close. I am simply saying that I knew I was loved, and her love empowered me.

Is there someone to whom you can express love? Don't miss the chance. It will probably bring love right back to you, and then two will be energized in the process.

Improves Our Self-Concept

If you feel unloved, actively express your love to others. Not only does it feel good to you, it also frees them to express love to you. "What goes around comes around."

Learn also how to express love to yourself. There is nothing wrong with loving yourself. The Bible teaches that we are to love others as we love ourselves. The one person in the world who will most likely take the best care of you is you. My friend, Gay Carlstrom, taught me this concept. She said she tells people to think of the most loving thing they can do for someone else and then do it for themselves.

Loving yourself is not selfish as long as your love does not stop with you. If we learn to love ourselves, we have a great reference point for loving others. A lot of people do not know how to express love to themselves. Following are some suggestions I have gleaned from friends and clients. These are specific ways you can express love to yourself.

- Call a friend.
- Take a walk in the woods or in a park.
- Go horseback riding.
- Get a massage.
- Soak in a bubble bath with a good book.
- Listen to some music you enjoy.
- Sit quietly and watch a sunset.
- Spend a day with a friend.
- Introduce yourself to a new experience.
- Buy yourself a gift.
- Take a day off and just see some sights.

The list can go on, but this will give you a few ideas to help you get started. Certainly one thing you can do is plan something nice for someone without expecting anything in return. Do it because you just want to do a nice thing. That too is a loving thing to do for yourself.

If you have everything else in the world but do not have love, it all adds up to nothing (1 Cor 13). If you are alive and breathing, you deserve to be loved. Even so, "deserving" has little to do with it. The fact is, you have as much value as anyone in the world. You don't have to earn it or prove it. You have value because you are a human being. Say it to yourself, "I am loved." Most of the time, all I really need to know is that I am loved. Just love me. Now abide these three faith, hope, and love. But, as the apostle Paul says, "The greatest of these is love."

The knowledge that I have been able to love someone and express that love in a practical and helpful way makes me feel better about myself. Jesus taught us to love even our enemies. That is not an easy task, but one that makes us feel better about ourselves.

A few years ago the church I served was voted out of a local convention because of a stand we had taken on a racial issue. We wanted to be on the cutting edge of improving racial relationships. It was easy to feel anger at people who did not understand our position. I read the following verse to our congregation. It became our prayer.

> Heretic, rebel, a thing to flout,
> They drew a circle and put us out.
> But love finds a way to win.
> We drew a circle and took them in.

Casts Out Fear

The love of God is expressed in the gift of His life for us. He so loved that He gave His only Son that we might have life through Him (John 3:16). Being loved that much motivates people to serve God by serving their fellow human beings. I first expressed my faith in God because I was afraid to live without that faith. The more I have learned about God, the less afraid I have become. I now serve God because I honestly love God. Service is more meaningful in my mind when it comes from love rather than from fear.

The little book of 1 John teaches that love casts out fear. It says that when we are afraid, it is evidence that we have not been perfected in love. There will always be a little fear in us because we will not reach perfection in this world. The fact is, however, the more love we have for life and people, the less we fear either one.

An awareness of the love of God can empower us even to face death with less apprehension. I recently visited with a lovely Christian lady who was dying. I asked her what image of God she had in her mind. She said she was picturing God lovingly holding her in His arms. She never stopped holding that image in her mind. She died peacefully, assuring her loved ones that she was not afraid. I am convinced that her awareness of God's love reduced her fear.

Maybe the power of love to ease our fears, help us make it through the tough times, and energize us is what led Jesus to say that the whole duty of mankind could be summed up in the commandment, "Love the Lord your God with all your heart and mind and soul, and love your neighbor as you love yourself."

Leads Us to Suffer for Others

I was on a train years ago. We were about to pull out of Union Station in St. Louis. A man, dressed in tattered clothing, was putting his family on the train to return to their home. I caught just enough of the conversation to know that he was remaining behind to look for work. He was going to send for them as soon as he was able.

He got off the train and stood on the platform looking at the window near which his family was seated. I watched him reach into his pocket and pull out some crumpled bills. He hurried back onto the train. He asked his wife if she was sure she had enough money to make it. She nodded. He was not convinced. I know he had tears in his eyes as he crumpled a couple of the bills into her hand. He said, "You take this. I have enough to get by."

She wanted to refuse, but she knew he was acting out of love. She nodded. They hugged each other. He hugged the two children and departed on the train. I watched him stand waving as we pulled out of the station.

Love motivated that man to give more than he could afford. Love motivates people to work, study, and give. Love is so strong as a bond and motivator that people have actually laid down their lives for their friends.

Makes Problem Solving Easier

It is a lot easier to walk through the fires of problem solving in an atmosphere of love than in an atmosphere of anger or resentment. I find it easier to solve problems with the people I love than with people whom I find hard to like. When we love someone, we are interested in being close to them. We want to resolve our differences and walk together.

The whole process of solving problems would be made easier if we would learn to love problem solving. Learn to frame problems in terms of challenges and desired results. This will change your feeling about difficulties and make it easier to work on them.

Practice Love

Begin to think of yourself as one who loves others. Say it to yourself. Write notes about it, and read them often. "I am a person who is loved, and I love others."

What does this mean? It means I am willing to be a friend to the people in my family and others around me. It means I will accept others and communicate that acceptance to them in whatever way I can. It means I will be vulnerable enough to let others get to know me. It means I will make myself available to others.

Such a lifestyle will empower me. I will love my own life more when I am loving others. I will be loved more when I am loving others. That awareness will help me walk through the fires of life with greater courage.

CHAPTER 17

Foundations
Build on the Rock

JESUS TAUGHT US TO BUILD OUR LIVES ON A SOLID FOUNDATION. HE said if we build on the sand, then the storms of life will beat on our house and it will fall. He further said if we build on the rock, our house will withstand the storms. No matter how good the superstructure, we must still have a solid foundation in order to stand during the storms. This is another way of saying we have to have a solid base of belief if we are to make it through the fires of life.

Jesus was talking about his own teachings. He said those who heard his teachings and obeyed them were building on the rock. The teachings of this book are not as powerful as the teachings of Jesus. But I believe they are consistent with what he taught. Even so, they form a superstructure. Each of us has to find the foundation within our own belief system. My foundation is my personal faith.

Healthy Spirituality

Healthy faith is an aid to health. Thomas Moore wrote in *Care for the Soul* that there can be no mental health without spirituality. He further pointed out that while healthy spirituality is good for the soul, there is also a brand of religion that creates compulsive and hostile behavior. We have for too long ignored such militaristic religion and in so doing have become accomplices to bad faith. That rigid and aggressive, often hostile, approach to the spiritual is not just an error. It is in and of itself evil and unhealthy.

Spirituality that leads to fear, excessive guilt, judgmental attitudes, hostility, rejection, prejudice, and anger is not healthy spirituality. Such approaches lead to the mentality that caused the misguided Jim Jones to lead hundreds of people to commit suicide as an act of faith. Such approaches to religion lead people to murder abortion clinic employees in the name of God. While healthy faith may lead you to oppose abortions, it will not lead you to become hostile and vindictive in the expression of your beliefs. That is not healthy socially or physically.

Healthy spirituality is grounded in love and acceptance. It is grounded in the desire to help people walk through their pain and become whole again. Healthy spirituality is personal. It always comes down to "What do you believe is the truth?" If it is healthy, then it will not harm others. Healthy faith is good enough to live with and die with, but healthy faith does not get in the way of health and wholeness.

I understand there will be differences of opinion as to what is healthy faith. It remains the responsibility of each one of us to pursue our own personal faith. I cannot claim to have arrived with perfect faith. Perfect anything is only an illusion in human experience. What I can do is share my own faith. It has been healthy for me.

My Personal Faith

I am a Christian. I have accepted Jesus Christ as resurrected Lord in my life. I have accepted him personally. I believe he is God's unique Son. My experience of him and my faith in him have been the source of strength in my life.

If my faith is healthy, it will certainly be reflected in the way I live my life daily. I will be a loving person. I will actively seek to follow the teachings of Christ. Healthy spirituality will enable me to admit that my life is not free of problems. My life has been filled with them, particularly as I grow older. I have fewer solutions and more questions about life, but I have found in my personal faith in Jesus Christ not only a Savior but a direction and a goal. Hebrews 12:1-4 calls him the author and finisher of our faith. He is my goal and example.

My faith in Jesus has enabled me to accept forgiveness for myself and extend it to others as often as I possibly can. My faith helps me believe that, somehow, everything is going to be alright. It gives me hope in my darkest hours and empowers me to share that hope with others.

The text of my life is Philippians 4:4-13. The mission of my life is to joyfully spend my life alleviating the pain of others. If my faith did not lead to a desire to alleviate suffering, extend love, practice forgiveness, and believe in hope, then it would not be healthy spirituality. Healthy spirituality is grounded in personal faith that motivates me to sing when I am hurting, celebrate even when I am grieving, hope against the darkness, walk through the fire, believe in life while dying, always give thanks, and find meaning through it all.

Establish Your Own Foundation

Each of us must build on our own foundation. We can learn from one another, but we still have to live our lives for ourselves. Much to my dismay, my oldest son used to say to me, "Dad, I respect your opinions, and I love you, but I have to make my own mistakes." He has. So have I. We all have to make our own mistakes and live our own lives. Decide on your own foundation. It must involve personal faith. You decide for yourself. When I recognize my foundation in God's grace, I can begin to build my creed on that foundation. My creed based on that faith follows.

> *I am a person who will persevere, in good times and bad. I will accept responsibility for myself, believing that somehow everything in life will eventually work out for good because of God's grace. I will maintain integrity with my real values. I will express gratitude for all the good I have received. I will maintain a sense of humor; it is my seventh sense. I love life. I love people. I love God. That leads me to live passionately and joyfully every day. Life is a celebration of God and my own uniqueness. I will patiently wait for the revelation of all that is good and all that is eternal. I determine my attitudes internally. I will take what is and make the most of it. I can then live with a sense of hope, and I know I will be able to cope through Him who strengthens me. I have no need to judge others. Each person has enough to answer for. I will encourage others to live out their own uniqueness, and I will alleviate suffering whenever I can.*

Bibliography

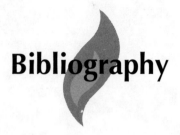

Biehl, Bob. *Stop Setting Goals.* Nashville TN: Moorings, 1995.

Clark, Glenn. *I Will Lift Up Mine Eyes.* San Francisco: Harper & Row, 1936.

Connellan, Thomas K. *How to Grow People into Self-Starters.* Ann Arbor MI: The Achievement Institute, Inc., 1988.

Covey, Stephen R. *First Things First.* New York: Simon & Schuster, 1994.

Little, Bill l. *This Will Drive You Sane.* Minneapolis MN: Comp/Care, 1977.

Mann, Gerald. *When the Bad Times Are Over for Good.* New York: McCracken Press, 1992.

Robbins, Anthony. *Unlimited Power.* New York: Faucett Columbine, 1986.

Senge, Peter M. *The Fifth Discipline.* New York: Currency Doubleday, 1990.

Swindoll, Charles R. *The Quest for Character.* Grand Rapids MI: Zondervan, 1982.

Sykes, Charles. *A Nation of Victims.* New York: St. Martin's Press, 1992.